by Frank Wappat

Dedicated to Chick's only child,
Lynda Ann

ACKNOWLEDGEMENTS

The author would like to thank the following people without whose invaluable help the book, relevant facts, and vital information would not have been available.

Pamela and Lynda Ann (Chick's widow and daughter).

The late Freda Rowntree (Chick's sister).

Arthur and Betty Smith (Betty is a niece).

Jean Erwin (another niece).

Jenny Keen (EMI Music Archives - Former BBC).

Bob Pace - Former Shipmate and friend of Chick.

Ted Rea - Dance Band Leader from Hartlepool.

Ian Charlton - BBC Radio Cleveland.

The following publications provided most useful information regarding Chick's vocals and life.

Brian Rust's Dance Band Discography (Harry Leader "Eclipses" and Columbia's).
Melody Maker (various quotes).
British Bandleaders' Club - (The London Piano Accordeon Band).
FWM Archives (Taped interviews with Joe Loss, Bob Pace, Chick's Widow and daughter, Chick's sister Freda, Photographs and letters written by Chick).
Stuart Dunkin Photographics (Blyth) and John Sampson (North Shields) re-photographed original photographs.

Susan MacGregor, my unpaid PA, and secretary, spent weeks typing up the information as it came in, often having to re-type it as additional data was made available. In some cases whole sections had to be subbed down (and often cut) as fresh information and proof contradicted information already held.

Without this dedicated work, the entire project could not have materialised in its present form.

Frank Wappat
North Shields
Tyne and Wear
NE30 2DL

CONTENTS

Published by Printability Publishing Ltd., Wolviston
Designed, Typeset and Printed by Atkinson Print Ltd.,
10/11 Lower Church Street, Hartlepool, Cleveland TS24 7DJ.
First Edition, December 1990.

ISBN 1 872239 04 8

PREFACE

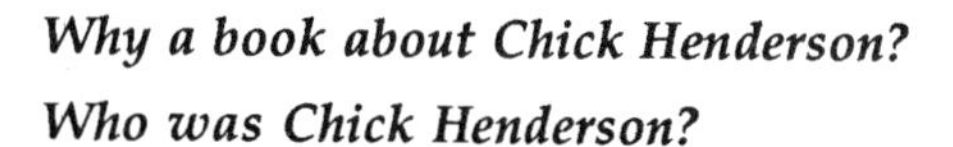

Why a book about Chick Henderson?

Who was Chick Henderson?

The answer to the first question is simple. The 1930's and 1940's were the golden years of the dance bands and crooners – a never to be forgotten worldwide phenomena. Popular songs of those days are the golden standards of today, simply because they had easily memorised melodies, usually built up of four sets of eight bars, with the second and fourth set being identical, and the first very similar, with only the middle eight being different, or thirty-two bars in total. The lyrics held an interesting tale, story, or eulogy. They were generally about love, in the polite caring sense – never about sexual intercourse – never vulgar – and they made a girl feel like a lady – a protected species, not something to be abused and ravished one night and discarded the next. Men were gentlemen in the lyrics, not male and female rapists, as later decades would reveal in so-called 'Pop' Tin Pan Alley.

Exponents in the vocal art of those far-off days were many – ten a penny to be precise. Good ones were rare. In the U.S.A., the undisputed 'King' was Bing Crosby. He had no equal, right through the Thirties. In the Forties, Dick Haymes, Frank Sinatra, Perry Como, and the Canadian 'Bing' – Dick Todd, came along as serious rivals, but they never took his crown. In this country in the 1930's, it seems that most vocalists or crooners as they were called, were imitation Bing Crosby's – high voiced Crosby's (Jimmy Mesene's early work including phrasing and trills) – low voiced Crosby's (Denny Dennis, in my opinion a copyist, in the 1930's although he has denied this). Chick's record of 'You started me dreaming' sounds like he is impersonating Denny Dennis!!

Al Bowlly – a South African by birth, came to England in 1928, and perfected a method of putting across a vocal where the microphone became the sole tool of his trade. His soft, unusually resilient voice could slide from chest to head without any break, and the close, almost whispered sound came out like "fine sandpaper soaked in treacle being gently rubbed down the spine" – as one fan put it. Bowlly disliked the word 'crooner', and described himself as a 'song stylist' – but crooner he was, in the accepted sense.

Chick Henderson, an unknown from Hartlepool, a town formerly in Durham County and now in County Cleveland, was a singer who took the part of a dance band vocalist – a crooner who was essentially a singer. He made his first record in June, 1935 and his last in January, 1942. His short recording career saw him leap in five years to Britain's No. 1 male singer – (In 1940 he was second top, Al Bowlly was fourth).

His early records were very ordinary indeed (he started at 23) but by his second year, at 25 years old, he had developed a rich manly voice, so unlike Crosby that he presented a refreshing and welcome change to the public at large – (compare his "Pennies from Heaven" to Bing's). The opportunity to prove himself came when the 64 bar song, "Begin the Beguine", was republished. (It had flopped in 1934). In July of 1939 Chick recorded it. It is still selling! It has become the best selling dance record ever made in the U.K. – a classic, and the definitive version of the song. Chick was more than a one hit wonder, too, as any new collector of his records will soon find out.

Who was Chick Henderson?

The fact that you may not know is the fault of the 'Pop' mad media who, for three decades, have denied the British their birthright in the form of their popular musical heritage. Americans have always re-issued from original masters, and continue to do so, the artistes and artistry of their Golden Age stars. In the U.K., the only two record companies we have with roots in the 20's and 30's, EMI and DECCA (Decca is now part of the Philips Group), **destroyed virtually every master and metalwork of their popular record catalogues.**

In 1968 I wrote the following . . .

"Who then is to blame for juvenile degradation? Who has reduced the noble British youth to a wriggling, trembling, shaking, twitching, convulsing conglomeration, of glassy eyed goons, whose very appearance, clothing and hairstyles, would scare the pants off any Dracula, Frankenstein Monster, or Horror Comic Zombie? The answer is simple – it is the chosen race of pop music purveyors – the greedy grasping gripes who first recorded the goulish gibberish of a few half-witted hairbrains, the absolute dregs of the bucket, possibly because they were too mean to pay musicians, and who labelled their quack, cheap concoction – "Pop Music" – and plugged it and pushed it over and over again into the gullible minds of the wanting-to-be different teenager – until the disease became an epidemic. Add to this a Foreign Legion of "Disc Jockeys", and Producers, some of whom would 'plug' their own grannies, for a back hander, then stir in one great big hypocrite which masquerades behind a blasé front of Olde English proprietry, but which underneath is in the swim up to its neck – dear old Auntie B.B.C., dilute with the not to "miss a buck" music publishers who would rock "Rock of Ages" and plug the "Lords Prayer" for a minute of "Air Time" then bring this hideous revolting mess of pottage slowly to the boil with an equally irresponsible ITV and the result – the youth of Today are whipped by this Jungle

Fantasy into a frenzy of wild cavortings followed closely by "punch-ups", kick-ups, knifings - wanton damage - rapings - immorality - plunderings, ad infinitum.

Our Missionaries will tell you that the most uncivilised of tribes can live peacefully for years until some fool strikes up the Tom Toms, and Rock and Twist Rhythms. Before long the whole tribe joins in, and within hours they start kicking, beating, killing, orgying and eating each other. A saying older than Christ that "music can bring the best out of a man" - is equally true in reverse.

The Dance Hall Hops of the 1930's with their Fox Trots, Waltzes, Quicksteps, and melodious melodies never produced the butchery and drunken hooliganism of the sizzling 60's with its Rock, Twist, Shout, Shake, Tremble and Quiver.

Having worked in the Dance Business before, during and after the advent of Rock 'n Roll, the writer was a first hand witness of the degenerative decline.

Never mind flogging the kids who disrupt - never mind cursing their irresponsible parents - leave the dithering old magistrates bellowing down each other's ear-trumpets, get at the root cause, cobalt bomb the cancerous roots - unsparingly slit with the scalpel - remove and burn the fat, rich un-British polluters - the hell-bound ship load of pop music purveyors - the Agents, the Managers, the Publishers, the Recording Chiefs, the B.B.C. and I.T.V. These are the destroyers of a Nation, those who manufacture and market, the jungle sounds and rhythms - and the Lyrics which pre-war would have earned the composers a life time in a padded cell.

The discreet "I kiss your little hand Madame" of 1932 has been replaced with "Come here I'm gonna have you tonight babe" in 1968 - and with it a once moral God fearing leader of the world - the British Lion - has been reduced to an immoral tenth rate state - The once "Roaring Lion" is now a moth eaten rug, on which all the 2½ d, tenth rate countries scornfully wipe their naked feet".

That article, incidentally, so impressed the senior B.B.C. producer at B.B.C. Newcastle, that he gave me my present job at the B.B.C. when he became Manager of B.B.C. Radio Newcastle in January, 1971.

In reading this book, however, you will learn a little about the exciting musical world of yesteryear - a world which the B.B.C. and I.B.A. have denied access to - for you and millions like you.

The B.B.C. has the biggest record collection in the world, and it keeps the doors firmly locked.

FRANK WAPPAT

ROOTS AND BACKGROUND

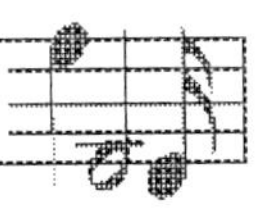

Chick Henderson's real name was Henderson Rowntree. It was an unusual forename, having served as a surname previously in the family tree. To his family and close friends he was known as "Hendy". He was born in the industrial North-East town of Hartlepool on 22nd November, 1912. When he met the girl that he eventually married, she asked him why he was called "Chick". He told her that he was one of nine children and the youngest boy. His mother hadn't planned for nine children – nor had she planned for him amongst six daughters and two other sons. When he was born, she had him Christened "Henderson" and, because he was small and in a large "brood", she referred to him as her "little chick" – (little chicken in a large brood of hens).

Little "Chick" stuck, so he became "Chick Henderson", though many and varied have been the theories offered by so many people – but that is how he said he got the name "Chick" – his mother called him that from the very beginning of his life. His family, however, had never heard the story . . . his first bandleader boss tells a different story later. He attended Galley's Field School – and certainly not St. Hilda's Church of England School, as others have said. He attended St. Hilda's Church Sunday School and later was a member of the Young Men's Bible Class.

One hundred years earlier, the population of Old Hartlepool was only around 1,000, whilst nearby Middlesbrough contained only 200 inhabitants. By the start of World War 2, the same area was to boast a population of around 200,000. The population was large, and so were the families. Young "Hendy's" six sisters were – Mary Elizabeth (known as "Tizzie"), Ethel, Hannah (known as Nan), Eva, Hilda and Freda – his brothers were Robert and Richard. The family home was at 62 Frederick Street, in what was known as 'Old' Hartlepool. Later, his parents moved to Raby Road, West Hartlepool. Today there is no 'Old' or 'West' Hartlepool. Both districts, plus other newer suburbs, have become simply the town of Hartlepool.

The Rowntree family were nominal Church of England members, although some of Hendy's sisters attended the Chapel, having as their favourite hymn tunes those assoicated with evangelical Christianity, such as "Sinking Sands" – otherwise known as "He lifted me".

Hendy's middle brother, Richard (Dick), was the exception. He spent some time in the Army, met a girl of Irish extraction who was a Roman Catholic, and, according to the custom of those days, he had to become a Roman Catholic and/or sign away any children, resulting from that union, to the Roman Catholic faith.

His son, Kevin Rowntree, became a radio and television interviewer, first for Metro Radio in Swalwell (although it insists it is in Newcastle upon Tyne, it is on the County Durham side of the River Tyne in Gateshead), and Tyne Tees Television.

Hendy had joined the Church of England (the Abbey Church of St. Hilda, Hartlepool) of his own choice, and when his singing voice came to the attention of the choir-master, he was asked to join the choir, which had quite a good musical reputation in the town. The evidence of voice training remained with Chick all his life. Good and correct breathing, controlled vibrato, and correct pitch and tuning, are evident on all of his recorded work. His interest in matters spiritual continued after he outgrew the Sunday School, and when his voice broke, he joined the Young Men's Bible Class under Canon F. T. Salter.

In later life, he continued to attend the Church of England in London, and wherever else his work took him.

Shortly after his marriage, he, his wife, Sandy McPherson the B.B.C. staff organist, Sandy's lady friend and another friend, came out of morning communion, and he lit a cigarette almost before he had stepped out of the Church door. His wife, seeing the humorous side of this action with his "Holy" smoke, photographed the four of them leaving the Church. In later years she exclaimed – "What a yob he looked, slouching away from Church with a cigarette in his mouth. Still, he liked his 'Craven A'," (a cigarette with an imitation tip – brown coloured paper around the end).

Chick (right) leaving Church one Sunday morning, Sandy McPherson, the famous broadcasting and recording organist, is second from the left. (The woman was Sandy's lady friend at that time).

All through his life he retained the habits and characteristics of his early life. He was very strong willed and determined, and he held positive views.

Once he had made his mind up, he was unshakeable.

He was very attractive to women – magnetic would be a better word, but unlike some of his contemporaries who loved their female fans in the fullest sense of the word, he had firm views on the female species. He put them on a pedestal and if they didn't live up to the standard he set for ladies, then they were fallen idols. Certainly, as his wife was to recall in 1990, "Chick put me on a pedestal and woe betide me if I ever tottered. He expected women to behave like ladies".

No matter which female tried to capture him in the years preceding his marriage, they were never allowed to interfere with his work, or try to talk him into quitting the Dance business.

In his own life, he was a very private person. Meticulous in personal matters, even to the extent of shyness or modesty, he was totally extrovert in other matters. He would sing anywhere – anytime.

Walking around the block one New Year's Eve to "first foot" the house, a relative recalled – "He sang every step of the way!"

His sense of humour was tremendous. He could get a laugh out of anything. He would often have friends and family in hysterics merely recounting the time his ship sank and he couldn't swim. Quite often he would lapse into pidgin English, Chinese or Indian when entering a bus, taxi, or restaurant. On other occasions, his wife recalled him talking loudly in the dialect of a Scot, or Welshman. Her embarrassment made him all the merrier, and keener to play even better japes. Once he took her to a restaurant – and walked in on his knees – pretending to be a midget.

Like many people who are basically shy and who live by a strong moral or ethical code, he had an extrovert side which lent itself beautifully to Showbusiness, and attracted admirers of both sexes by the hundred. He had beautiful, expressive eyes – and a beautifully expressive spirit which manifested itself in his artistic faculties. He was, from his earliest schooldays, a good "drawer" as they said in those days. Sketching came naturally to him. On one occasion he sketched his wife's hand with a pencil. It had a life-like quality, and often he took to sketching people's hands. He loved painting – and in his own style he was an accomplished artist.

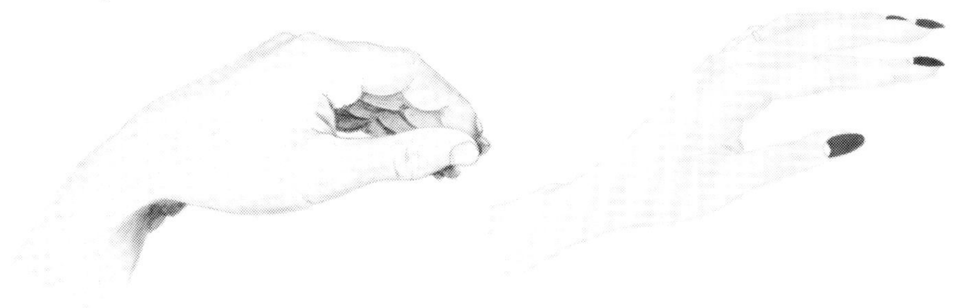

Sadly, very, very little of his work remains. Strange to say, his only child has this same flair for sketching.

He was courteous, charming, never crude, but – there again – never prudish. In a letter to a shipmate with its "buggers" and "bastards" and other bits of the vernacular, the meanderings ended with – "and don't forget to say a prayer now and again!" – and he meant what he said, and lived accordingly.

His Chaplain at the time of his Naval service described him as a "splendid fellow, and one we can ill do without these days". On "survivor's leave", he learned of the death by enemy action of Ken 'Snakehips' Johnson, and, two weeks later, Al Bowlly. Forgetting his own traumatic experiences, he journeyed to London to attend their funerals, whilst many parts of the Capital were wrecked and smouldering ruins.

He was only in the 'flesh-clothed' world for such a short while – yet his was, and still is, a shining spirit.

Henderson Rowntree was a special man when he was here and yet it is doubtful if his mum and dad saw anything different in him in those first years of his life.

THE ROWNTREE FAMILY
(The parents of Chick Henderson are on the right. His sister Freda is beside them circa 1923).

'THE EARLY YEARS'

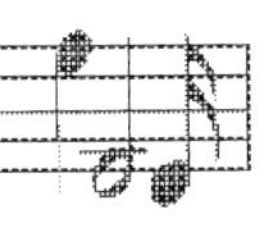

His early formative years were no different from those of thousands of other young lads at the time. He was nearly two years old when the First World War broke out, and at its total conclusion, early in 1919, he was only a six year old, and too young to be aware of the economic situation which was to bring unemployment, poverty, hunger and starvation until, when he reached his 19th birthday, there were over three million people unemployed – and at a time when the population was less than half of what it would be 50 years later.

The poverty of the 1930's was unbelievable in the industrial North of England, but it brought out the best in a community spirit. Folk who had any food left after a Sunday lunch, for example, would take it to a neighbour who was less well off. The writer remembers an old lady neighbour bringing in to his home whatever rice pudding was left over from her Sunday dinner (lunchtime on Sundays was a "dinner" time and the main meal of the day).

In 1933, as "Hendy", Rowntree's apprenticeship ended, so did his job, as the economic depression swept the North. He was unemployed for about twelve months. Singing kept his spirits buoyant.

Popular songs of the day were about exotic places, such as Hawaii, Mexico, Madrid, the Rocky Mountains – and prairies, cowboys, ranches and so forth . . .

Economic depression, poverty and hunger were regarded (in popular songs) as quite normal and acceptable, in such numbers as "We've got the moon and sixpence – and bread and cheese and kisses!" or "Just a little room, or two, would more than do, a little man and wife. We could be so happy with the little things in life".

Chick Henderson had always enjoyed singing and he knew all of the popular songs of the day from an early age. Every village and town

Chick's first official 'handout' photograph 1936

boasted more than one dance band. The better bands featured vocalists, whilst others often afforded an opportunity to known good singers to do the job, voluntarily on occasion.

Hartlepool lads and lasses visited their "Tanner Hops" – (a "tanner" being the admission fee – the equivalent of six old pence, or 2½p in today's currency – "Hop" being a slang word for a public dance). Their town, however, boasted a ballroom, as well as the usual Church Halls, Community Centre Rooms, or Labour Party huts. The Rink, to give the ballroom its correct title, was a large spacious converted skating rink, hence its name – and the town of Sunderland, 30 miles north, boasted a similarly named ballroom.

When local youths reached the age of eighteen or so, they graduated to the Rink Ballroom. Chick was one of them. Having acquired a reputation as a good "crooner", he was allowed to sing his favourite songs there. In February 1934, a new song was published, called "I'll be faithful, I'll be true". For some reason, the song is not listed in Leslie Lowe's "Directory of Popular Music", and this book is regarded by some as the song title Bible. The number was extremely popular, and the recording by Bertini and the Tower Ballroom Dance Band, made for Woolworth's "Eclipse" label in January 1934, sold far in excess of the usual 5,000 pressings maximum of the average dance band of the day.

Joe Loss recorded the song with his Band, for Edison Bell, and Jimmy Mesene took the vocal. Chick Henderson took a liking to the song, probably having bought the Bertini version on "Eclipse". It became his 'pièce de résistance'.

B.B.C. AUDITION

At that time he took a very bold step. He applied to the B.B.C. for an audition. He received a reply from the Newcastle Studio in New Bridge Street. At that time, B.B.C. Newcastle had around 30 minutes "air time" a day – an opt out from the National Service. Chick was invited to attend an audition. He went – but the myopic producer rejected him. He was devastated!

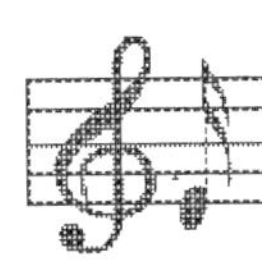

HOW CHICK WAS DISCOVERED

Blyth born bandleader, Ted Rea, had a 12 piece band which played at the Borough Hall, Hartlepool, the Queen's Rink, West Hartlepool, the Ice Rink, Spennymoor, and various Miners' Welfare Halls around Durham County. The Band was known as Ted Rea and his All-Star Syncopators.

Ted knew "Hendy" Rowntree from choir days at St. Hilda's Abbey Church, and, one Sunday evening after Evensong, there was a knock at his door. On opening it, Ted was surprised to see Chick standing there. "Ted, I'd like to be a dance band singer," said Chick. "Is there any chance of joining your Band?" he asked.

"Well," said Ted, taken aback a little – "why not come to our rehearsals on Tuesday night? We meet upstairs in the "Big" room at 7.30 p.m. in the North Eastern Hotel in Lynn Street." Not to be disappointed, Chick persisted. "Can't you give me a "run-over" now on your piano?" A little amused by the insistence, Ted invited him into the sitting room.

"What would you like to sing?" he asked.

"Well, I'd like to try that new one which is quite popular right now," answered Chick. "It's called, 'I'm heading for the last roundup'."

"Ah, yes," replied Ted. "I've got a copy of the sheet music here somewhere. Do you sing copy key?" he queried.

"I'll try," answered Chick.

Ted recalled in July 1990 . . .

"He had a very nice voice, rich and manly despite his youth – and a slight build. I asked him to come to the very next rehearsal so that the boys in the Band could hear him and also to see how he would fit in tempo-wise, etc. A good voice is one thing, a sense of rhythm is essential, and both must go together. It became very apparent after the first run through that young Hendy, or Chick, as he

On tour with Jan Ralfini's Band 1934

became later, took to the Band and the Band took to Chick, like a duck to water. From that moment, he joined the Band and became my regular vocalist!"

Ted Rea supplied vital information which refutes other accounts on what followed. He continued – "We had a Moss Empire Theatre in West Hartlepool, and the "Hippodrome". These theatres featured Variety Shows, and many of the popular Radio Dance Bands of the day. One particular week, Jan Ralfini and his Band appeared at the "Hippodrome", featuring what they called a Grand Talent Spotting Contest. Hendy was determined to enter, acquired and filled in the necessary entry form and was asked to appear on the opening night, which was Monday."

He sang his 'pièce de résistance' – "I'll be faithful" and won the heat outright. His reception was so fervent that the wise Ralfini asked him to "guest" every night. He agreed, and took the show by storm.

Naturally he won the final, and the leader asked him if he would like to join the Band. Absolutely overjoyed, he decided to accept the offer.

So it was, that, within three weeks, he joined Jan Ralfini for the rest of his tour, and summer season, playing at the Pier, Rhyl, in North Wales.

Young Hendy made many friends and fans there, especially amongst the females who clamoured to see him and talk to him before and after the Shows. One evening after the Show, one of these young girls brought him a hot, freshly cooked chicken for his supper. This strange gift became a joke, so much so that the lads in the Band started to call him "Chicken" – or the shortened pet form, "Chick"!

However, to "win" an opportunity to sing with a band of this calibre was a dubious honour, not to mention the risk involved from a financial angle alone. It was indeed to give Chick cause for concern later. Dance Bands and ballrooms were regarded as the breeding grounds of tuberculosis by many people. This disease killed thousands of people of all ages in those days, and in its most virulent form was known as "galloping consumption". Chick was warned that his health would be in danger and he would never know what would happen once he got there. His family had great confidence in his ability, not only as a singer, but also in his determination and ambition as a man.

At home he was much loved – handsome, charming, lovable and, in particular, a "great laugh". All age groups loved to be in his company. He had a good sense of humour – and loved to mimic people, impersonating the more flambuoyant, and imitating all manner of characters, both real and imaginary. He was to be a great loss as he packed his bags and left. However, he was not alone in his migration. Many other North-Easterners left to join the move South – where there had always been greener grass, if not more lucrative employment. Very few of the inhabitants of the North East had ever been to the capital of their country. The very rail fare itself was more than a week's wage to a labourer or unskilled worker.

Ralfini, real name Ralph Goodliffe, once claimed that he wanted a Latin type stage name when he began recording, just like Geraldo, who was Gerald Bright, so he added 'ini' to his forename to make it "Ralfini" – Jan was another bit of foreign addition. The story cannot be quite true, as he began recording before Geraldo – and Bertini.

Ralfini was not a big time dance band leader. His first gramophone records were made in 1926 for the Crystalate Company's "Imperial" label.

They were all rejected.

Three years later he recorded for "Parlophone".

These titles were rejected too.

One session for Columbia's "Regal" label was issued but no option was taken up on any more.

In 1930, Ralfini began recording for Crystalate's 7 inch "Victory" label, which were made exclusively for Woolworth's. Once again, he never received an invitation to make any more for them, but in 1931 and 1932, "Sterno" records gave him regular recording work. Aural evidence indicates one trumpet and trombone, three reeds and rhythm, with Jan Ralfini leading on a violin – as so many not so good musician-bandleaders did. Vocals were taken by London session men such as Tom Barratt.

At the time of his Hartlepool visit, his recording days had almost ended. His musicians were virtually all unknown. An attempted recording comeback in 1938 for EMI resulted in all of the recordings being scrapped once again. Although Ralfini was never offered a recording contract after 1935, he continued to lead a band until the 1960's, and died in April, 1976. At the time of his visit to Hartlepool, he was 36 years old.

Chick (left) with Bill Boland trombonist with the Joe Loss Band, Blackpool 1938

Chick had joined Jan Ralfini and his Band in April, 1934, and completed the Ralfini tour with the Band before they settled in North Wales for the summer season. At rehearsals, he became very uneasy as he overheard conversations about the bandleader, job prospects, and money. To him, Ralfini was an established radio and recording artiste – known quite well even in Hartlepool. He was not to know that Ralfini's recording days were numbered – that he had never been among the top ten bandleaders and that his gramophone records didn't sell.

It was rumoured by some members of the Band that Ralfini's talent contests were a mere front to attract the sort of crowds that he could not get on his musical merits. Others said that he was searching genuinely for a star vocalist to put his Band back on the map. This is not borne out by any foresight on his part, for Chick had everything a leader could need – even the ability to make the only million selling gramophone record a pre-war Britain was to hear. To make gramophone records meant a greater possibility of getting broadcasts. Broadcasts meant engagements in nightspots, and invitations to appear in Variety Theatre.

It seems obvious, upon reflection, that Ralfini was having difficulty meeting recording standards. A final disagreement six months later over wages and alleged non-payment, resulted in five members of the Band quitting and walking out at the end of the summer season at Rhyl. Chick joined them – so the complaints must have been quite serious and well founded – especially when Ralfini did nothing to try and persuade Chick to stay. The six men were fortunate as a group, because they heard that a Dutchman called Louis de Vries, who had come to England, wanted to form an all English Band, to tour and record. They approached him, auditioned, and they all got the job!

Dutch trumpet star Louis de Vries

De Vries was a well known 'hot' trumpet player who hailed from Holland. He made a name for himself as lead trumpet in the "Original Ramblers" – a Dutch outfit of seven, headed by Theo Uden Masman on piano. It is to be greatly regretted that, although de Vries made records under his own name in the jazz style of the 1930's, he doesn't get a listing or a mention in Charles Delaunay's Hot Discographies – nor is he mentioned in Brian Rust's Dance or Jazz Discographies, despite the fact that English Decca issued the following in 1935:

F.5566	St. Louis Blues / Moon Glow
F.5658	Oh, you sweet thing / I cover the waterfront

– all four titles being listed as by Louis de Vries and his trumpet.

Although he started out with the "Original Ramblers" (the band became simply "The Ramblers") the Band did not record until 1932, according to Albert McCarthy's "Dance Band Era", where its first session took place for 'Decca' in the Chenil Galleries. De Vries was not present.

This is not true, for the Band first recorded in 1929 for HMV and "Odeon".

His first recorded evidence with the Band is in Holland on 13th August, 1935, when the Band featured him in three of his own arrangements.

AM.174-2 Oh, you sweet thing
AM.175-2 Rhythm is our business
AM.176-3 With all my heart and soul
De Vries does not appear on Matrices 177/8/9/180/1.

On this session, the recording files show Louis de Vries as the leader of the Band instead of Masman, and the recordings appeared as by "Louis de Vries and his Rhythm Boys", despite the fact that Masman is present and plays!

English 'Decca' F.5658 contains track 1 above, "Oh, you sweet thing".

The "Rhythm Boys" were:

George Van Helvoirt	–	second trumpet
Marcel Thielmans	–	trombone
Wim Poppink	–	clarinet, alto, baritone sax
Andre van der Ouderas	–	tenor sax
Theo Uden Masman	–	piano
Jac Pet	–	guitar
Lion Groen	–	bass
Kees Kranenburg	–	drums

These titles are omitted, together with the English 'Decca' items before them, from "Index to Jazz". Brian Rust doesn't mention the Ramblers English or Dutch recordings.

The reason English 'Decca' issued the two 78 rpm discs was to coincide with visits that year to England of the Dutch star player, who decided to stay over here and form a Band of his own. Principally this was to provide a showcase for his own trumpet playing. He had advertised the fact just at the time that the six Ralfini lads decided to quit.

This proposed band never actually materialised. De Vries was killed outright in a tragic motoring accident, leaving the five musicians and Chick without any job prospects, or money with which to pay for accommodation. Chick, however, had been on very friendly terms with his previous bandleader, Ted Rea in Hartlepool.

Ted and his fiancee (who became his wife later) attended the Baptist Chapel at Hartlepool, whilst Chick was courting a girl named Frances

(Francey) Sanderson, at St. Hilda's Church of England Church. The four of them often socialised together when the band was not playing. Consequently, Chick knew that Ted's parents were moving to Slough, in Berkshire.

He remembered this as he visited Archer Street in London. This street was famous as a meeting place for musicians and singers who were seeking work or fancied a change of Band. Vocalists were ten a penny at that time, so there appeared little chance of any immediate work for Chick.

He wrote to Ted, explained his dilemma, and asked if he would see if his parents could put him up as a boarder, reasoning that if he had a base, even at Slough, he could travel into Town (London) each day to continue to look for work. Ted's parents were happy to agree, and so Chick moved in with them. Travelling into London each day cost money, and money was in short

Eddie Pratt (left) Lead Alto saxophonist in the Joe Loss Band, an oyster seller on Blackpool's Golden Mile and Chick – braces and all! 1938

supply. He confided to a "Radio Pictorial" journalist in April 1937, that he had been so ashamed of not being able to pay his board and lodgings, that he slept rough in Trafalgar Square on one occasion.

He decided to sign on at the Employment Exchange at Slough. 'Dole' money, liable to be stopped after a matter of weeks in those days, could provide the bus fares to London, and perhaps a sandwich or two, as he wandered from agent to agent, and followed up leads which generally led nowhere at all. It was October, and Christmas 1934 was going to be a very bleak time indeed if he didn't find a job as a singer.

The totally bleak outlook was averted in the nick of time!

Having registered at the "Dole" in Slough as a time-served Marine Engineer, a vacancy arose in the local factory of Hi-Duty Alloys Ltd. Chick was given a card to go along for an interview as an engineering fitter.

Although his heart was in singing, he had no option but to go for the interview. To refuse this would have meant the end of the meagre unemployment benefit and the means of contributing to the cost of his lodgings.

To the Engineering Company, his appearance at the interview was a gift not to be questioned – A North-Easterner, time-served in Marine Engineering, was a rare bonus to a factory in Slough. He was given the job and started work immediately at his old trade as an engineer.

At the factory, he fitted in well, making friends quite easily because of his happy and humorous outlook on life.

Naturally, he went to the local dance halls and continued to follow the hit songs and dance bands of the day on the radio. Some evenings, and Saturdays, he continued to visit Archer Street in London, in the hope that he could find regular work as a dance band singer.

Christmas 1934, and New Year 1935, passed uneventfully, and his work at the factory provided much needed cash, most of which he saved. During holidays, he was able to spend each day in London searching for vocal work. His grit and determination paid off.

At that time, Bandleader (aptly named) Harry Leader, was beginning to make a name for himself, putting out two or three outfits in and around London for various kinds of functions.

Chick had approached him before, but this time he was successful. Leader auditioned him at his London office and signed him up to sing with his Band there and then.

It was an open contract in effect. It left Chick free to accept any other vocal work when not actually singing with the Harry Leader Bands. As vocal work was evening work, he continued as long as he could working as an engineer by day.

HARRY LEADER

Leader's background was a lot more solid than that of Ralfini. He was a saxophone player, fresh on the recording scene, having made his first recordings in May of 1933 for the 'Decca' group, with three reeds, two trumpets, one trombone, four rhythm, and session vocalist Sam Browne. His first B.B.C. broadcast was given him that year for the Overseas service of the B.B.C. The following year he was networked in the U.K. (It is claimed that his career ended in 1967, but in fact he made a comeback with a stereo LP in 1972 especially for dancing, for it included contemporary recordings of quicksteps, foxtrots, waltzes and sequence dances.

In November 1933, Harry Leader achieved his biggest break as the No. 1 named bandleader on Crystalate's recently launched "Eclipse" label, especially for Woolworths. All in all he made 140 records for this label. Some were made under pseudonyms such as "Joe Taub and his Melodians", the "Connecticut Collegians", and "Lew Sylva" – (a pun on Lou Gold, the American leader). He made the fastest selling 78 rpm disc of the early 1930's, a continuous run of 48,000 copies of "Little Man, you've had a busy day" – Matrix 1973-1 and 2 on "Eclipse" No. 729. The un-named vocalist was Dan Donovan! He used some of the best musicians and singers in the U.K., including Billy Farrell from Blaydon-on-Tyne on trumpet, Freddy Gardner on saxophone/clarinet, Charlie Smart on Wurlitzer organ, George Rowe - trombone, and Billy Amstell - clarinet/saxophone. Vocalists included – Sam Browne, Phyllis Robbins, Bill Airy-Smith, Les Allen, Brian Lawrence, Jack Lorrimer, Val Rosing, Dawn Davis, Dan Donovan, Alan Kane, and Clarence Wright.

HARRY LEADER

After the war, though, he and his Band were "banned" by the B.B.C. because the B.B.C. claimed "it was not up to standard". It was to be some time before he was allowed to broadcast again. Nevertheless, the pre-war outfit was a force to be reckoned with, and to his prize roster of some of Britain's best artistes in their field of popular music, the name of Chick Henderson was added for his very first gramophone record, on the 15th June, 1935. Matrix 2544-1 "Eclipse" catalogue No. 1011 – "Zing went the strings of my heart" was the title. However, it was the third title of the session, "Little Golden Locket", Matrix No. 2546-1 "Eclipse" No. 1010, which was issued first. Two months afterwards, in August 1935, Bandleader Bobby Howell was given a broadcast by the B.B.C. It was he who gave Chick his first broadcast.

BOBBY HOWELL AND JOE LOSS

Bobby Howell was one of the beneficiaries under the B.B.C.'s change of musical policy. Having been convinced by some that the top favourite bandleaders such as Lew Stone, Roy Fox, Harry Roy, Ambrose, Carroll Gibbons, etc., had a monopoly and unfair advantage, the B.B.C. introduced a disastrous new policy which took the top bands off the air and gave their prime

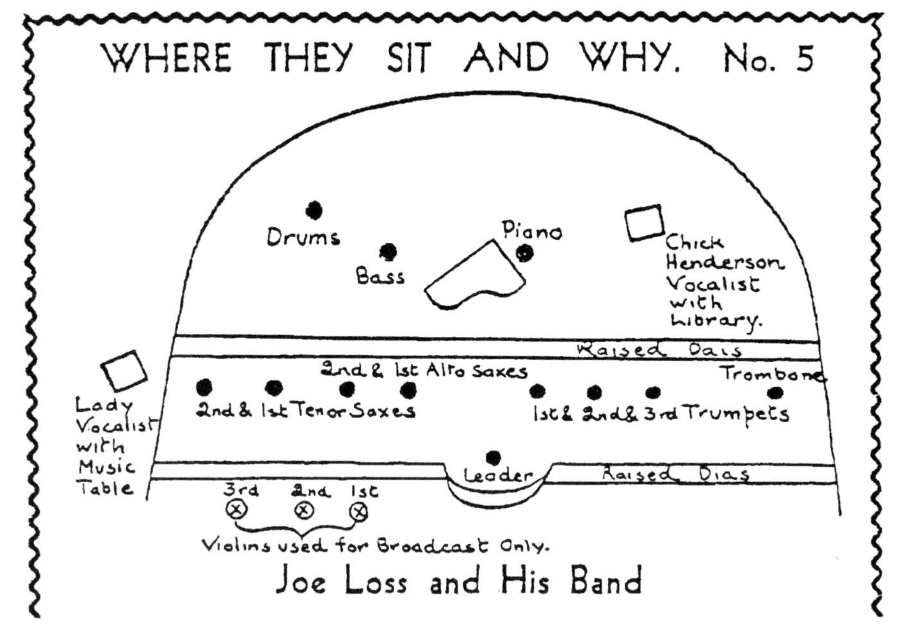

Explanation: "I like my 1st trumpet next the saxes so that they can hear him," says Joe Loss. "For broadcasts, I use three violins and place them directly in front of the saxes. For an ideal layout, I would have the brass behind the saxes, but the rostrum is not deep enough.

"Chick Henderson is on the stand and has a table with the library near him, so that if I need an arrangement quickly he can look it out for me on the spot. Marjorie Kingsley, my lady vocalist, has a chair off the stand, with a table for her music."

Personnel: Joe Loss (director); Eddie Pratt (1st alto), Danny Miller (2nd alto), Reg Brewster (1st tenor), Micky Lewis (2nd tenor); Harry Letham (1st trumpet), Bill Burton (2nd trumpet) and Clem Stevens (3rd trumpet); Bill Boland (trombone); Harry Kahn (piano, arranger); Jackie Greenwood (drums); Reg Richman (brass); violins—Oscar Grasso, George Hurley and Len Lee (broadcasts only); vocalists—Chick Henderson and Marjorie Kingsley. On broadcasts, vocalist Monte Rey is added.

time to new and often virtually unknown Bands which did not always possess well rehearsed, slick, star quality musicians and vocalists.

Bobby Howell, who made only one set of dance band gramophone records ever, using unknown musicians, fitted into the new policy, despite the fact that he liked, recorded, and broadcast Light music! He was of course, essentially a Cinema musical director who used a very large aggregation for this type of work. His variety work, using all kinds of Acts was at many of the theatres and other venues owned by the Gaumont British Entertainments Group of cinemas, ballrooms, and other similar establishments. He survived until 1962. On his B.B.C. broadcast in 1935, Howell used a dance band type of orchestra. In true Hollywood style, we're told that Joe Loss was listening quite conveniently to the radio when Howell made that broadcast - liked the voice of the lad from Hartlepool, and invited him to talk to him about his future.

Joe Loss had just ended his short recording contract with Octacros, and was hoping to secure a contract with the giant EMI group.(Octacros was a label so obscure outside of London that the writer has never seen one in all of the thousands which have passed through his hands).

Chick playing 'dummy' guitar, Joe Loss (front right) expected more from a top vocalist than songs. Chick had to sit and pretend to be a musician too.

Not unnaturally, Loss was very impressed with Chick, whose manly voice and good looks were both in stark contrast to his previous male vocalist, Jimmy Mesene. However, Chick was under contract to Harry Leader, and Harry was not very pleased at the thought of Joe trying to take his star male vocalist. Harry's contract with Crystalate's "Eclipse" had ended with Chick's first recording session. Because of this, plus the fact that his future was a little uncertain, he was prepared to release Chick from his contract, provided that if he got another recording contract himself, Joe would allow Chick to continue recording for the Harry Leader organisation. Joe Loss agreed and proved his integrity when Harry Leader procured a contract with EMI's "Columbia" label three months later, in September, 1935. Chick recorded the very first number, which was "You're all I need" (Columbia FB 1144).

EMI used odd pseudonyms for their budget label Regal-Zonophone and Harry, as well as Joe Loss, fell victim to these. "Mel Rose and his Orchestra" and "Wally Bishop and his Band" being two of them. Chick appeared on these too.

Chick's final break with Harry Leader came on the session dated 15th March, 1938, thus ending a three year association between Harry Leader and Chick Henderson, the duration of the original contract. I read elsewhere that Harry Leader "managed" Chick and that Chick never paid him his 10%. On behalf of Chick's family, I would like to refute this allegation. Harry Leader may have "managed" Chick whilst he was in his employment – in which case he controlled Chick's income too, and would deduct whatever money he felt due to him. When Joe Loss engaged him, he bought him out, and it was on the understanding that Harry Leader could still use him for recording and broadcasting for the three year period for which he had previously signed Chick. If money had been owed to Leader, I cannot imagine him paying recording and broadcasting fees to Chick without deducting what was owed to him. The story that Chick agreed to perform with Leader's Band in 1940 on a B.B.C. broadcast to make up for the amount owed is absolute rubbish. Chick's fee for broadcasting was £2!! That they – Leader and Henderson "revived" "Begin the Beguine" for that session is totally untrue. The original recording was issued in September 1939, so a "revival" six months later would have been a joke – the record was still being pressed at the rate of 4,000 a month, and the song lived on as a hit until Chick's untimely death in 1944. It most certainly never needed a "revival", and Joe Loss continued to feature it using Harry Kaye as the vocalist until Kaye left him. Loss's Band continues to feature it in the 1990's under its new conductor.

LONDON – WITH THE No. 1 BAND OF THE No. 1 LABEL - "HIS MASTER'S VOICE"

Two months after his Octacross recording session in August 1935, (which, incidentally, featured a young girl vocalist named Vera Lynn!) Joe Loss signed the contract with EMI which was to last longer than that of any other bandleader in the world. From October 1935, until his death in 1990, Joe Loss remained with the same company. A record in recording of 55 years!

His first recording for EMI featured Chick, and appeared on the HMV BD "Variety" series (BD 100) which began the year before the "Dance" (BD 5000) series. "Wyoming in the gloaming" was the obscure first title, of four which were cut on 22nd October, 1935 (Matrix OEA 1998-1 Catalogue No. BD 293). The records didn't sell very well but, nevertheless, at 25 years of age, Joe had become the No. 1 Bandleader for Europe's No. 1 label. HMV was such an important label that only specially selected dealers were allowed to sell them. Funnily enough, this did not restrict sales – it increased them, and only the best artistes in their profession were ever meant to get on the label.

In the previous five years, the British Dance Band scene had been dominated by "Society" Dance Bands – bands which played for the rich and royal – in fact, Royalty! . . . . Lew Stone at the Monseigneur Restaurant, Piccadilly – Roy Fox at the Kit Kat Club – Ambrose – then Harry Roy at the Mayfair – Sydney Lipton at the Grosvenor then the Dorchester Hotel. All of these bands had "star" sidesmen amongst their musicians and singers. Lew Stone could boast Joe Crossman, Europe's top reed man, as well as Nat Gonella, trumpet, and Lew Davis, trombone. Roy Fox had Denny Dennis, trumpeter Sid Buckman, and saxist Harry Gold, whilst Ambrose at the Embassy had Max Goldberg - trumpet, Ted Heath - trombone, Danny Polo - clarinet, and Max Bacon - drums.

Joe Loss did not have a Society Band with name sidesmen. His was a "Palais" Band – a Dance Hall Band . . . a band made for dancing for Joe Public who could outstep any of the "toffs" at the Society gigs who shuffled and pranced in the narrow spaces left between the tables of guzzling gourmets who could afford a meal costing up to five times the weekly wage of a Northern pitman.

The Astoria Dance Salon off Charing Cross Road was where the best dancing of that day took place with the quite nondescript group of musicians who worked for Joe Loss. However, they had the knack of bouncing a "lift" which could make people dance. To be strictly fair, a lot of this was the result of Joe's good, steady drummer, Jack Greenwood, who, with Reggie Richmond - string bass, drove the band along. (Greenwood stayed with Loss for 20 years!) Later, in 1936 Jack Hylton returned to the U.K. and resumed his place as HMV's No. 1 Band. Joe had got the No. 1 position because of Jack's absence. Joe was relegated to Regal-Zonophone, EMI's budget price label. This meant that more people were able to purchase his records. Increased sales brought increased popularity and, more so, to his handsome crooner who was responsible for a hard core of new young ladies at the Astoria, which, in turn, attracted more young men. This fact alone increased record sales.

THE WOMEN IN CHICK'S LIFE

In April 1937, Chick spoke about his love life to a "Radio Pictorial" journalist. Of course the journalist wasn't interested in homely stories of canny Hartlepool lasses, so before reprinting the 'London' line, it is relevant to consider first of all the Hartlepool girls.

Chick courted, as mentioned earlier, Francey Sanderson, Frances died in the 1980's. She was a dainty, petite young girl, and their relationship lasted quite a while. On one occasion, after a disagreement, he began courting a girl named Josie Hogg, but he claims to have 'dropped' her, and returned to Francey. Josie may have been the one who told him to get a "proper" job, when he applied to the B.B.C. for an audition.

His mike is his sweetheart –
Chick Henderson in full swing.

Chick himself takes up the story . . . .

"I'd been looking for work for twelve months, having served my apprenticeship as a Marine Engineer. But I didn't want to be an engineer. I wanted to sing. And I flopped . . . .

"Get a real job" – the girl had said – "and I'll marry you." If only she had taken my hand before I went into that studio, and said: "Good luck – I know you'll get through," well, I might have had a chance. Instead, she laughed.

So I broke my next date with her, to sing in a "gig" and I never saw her again. Who cares?

I wouldn't "come down to earth."

The next woman I nearly fell in love with also laughed at the wrong moment. We met at a ball – she was a guest, and I'd just got a night's job singing in the band. She drove me home afterwards, and there was a full moon, and we rather liked each other. She asked me where I worked, and I told her I didn't, whereupon she mentioned that her father owned a chain of shoe-stores.

I explained that I had ambitions to be a singer. She laughed, a social little laugh, and told me to "come down to earth." I did.

I took my arm from around her waist, stepped out of the car, raised my somewhat battered hat, and frigidly said: "Good-night." What I really meant was: "Good-bye!"

One day I took part in a local talent competition, Jan Ralfini heard me, and I was offered a job in his band. Simultaneously I was offered a job at sea. A girl whom I had known for some years – a schooldays sweetheart – advised me to take the job at sea. I packed my trunks immediately and went – to Jan Ralfini.

Why *wouldn't* these women understand?

Singing with Jan Ralfini one week at Birmingham, a beautifully gowned and obviously wealthy young lady came round to the stage door one night and asked to see me. Maybe she was crazy, but she was sweet, too.

She told me she had quite fallen in love with my voice. I escorted her home, and after that – well, we saw quite a lot of each other. Here was a girl who understood me all right, and didn't laugh in the wrong places.

It was too bad that her parents were so old-fashioned. It appeared that they harboured the gravest suspicions of anybody connected with the stage . . . and when they discovered that I was a singer, fireworks started immediately! I was told that unless I took to a "respectable job" I must stop seeing their daughter.

Did I tell you that girl was sweet? She was brave too . . .

We had one more meeting, secretly, and it turned out to be our last. "You mustn't let me stop you, you mustn't let me stand in your way," she said. And she told me how it was with her – how she was going to hate losing me – "hate it like the dickens." But yet, if I were to give up singing, so that I could be with her still, then I would not be the same man she had known and liked so much.

She said: "I know you are too strong to let a woman interfere with your work. You are set on an idea. Well, that's all right with me. I understand. And I dream of the day when I shall be sitting at home, and I shall suddenly hear your voice on the air. . . ."

I have never seen or heard of her from that day to this, but I always wonder if she is still listening.

Yes, I've made some grand friends – and I've had to say goodbye to them.

There was, for instance, a girl vocalist in another band which I joined for a while. She was just a pal, but we went around together quite a lot that is, until the leader pointed out she was *his* girl friend.

I knew then, from the way he spoke, that if there were any "big breaks" going in *that* particular outfit, it would be she who would get them. I didn't want to stand in her way, and I couldn't let her stand in mine.

I decided to quit immediately. It was an unexpectedly tearful parting. She said: "Listen, boy, you don't want to walk out like this, you're a stranger to London. Suppose I come with you, and we try a double act."

I told her she was a darling: "But whose girl friend *are* you, anyway?" I said, and that was the end of that.

NIGHTS IN TRAFALGAR SQUARE

It was certainly tough, being out of work in London, but I reckoned that "he travelled fastest who travelled alone." And when I got ashamed of not being able to pay my rent – well, I could always go out and sleep a couple of nights in Trafalgar Square!

I couldn't let a girl do that – but I did it!

Every time I go on the air there's a girl on my mind, and the memory of her helps me as I sing. She's a girl who does not laugh at the wrong moment!"

Chick third from the left with members of the Joe Loss Band.

CHICK HENDERSON FRIENDSHIP CIRCLE

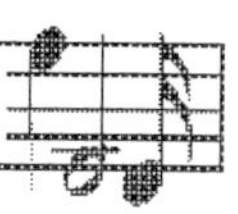

Soon, letters like this appeared in the entertainment magazines.

"Would you give me a few details about Chick Henderson, please? His age, if he is married, and any hobbies he may have". – *J. L., Darlington.*

As a rule we are not allowed to publish the ages of the stars, unless they reveal them to us personally. However, Chick Henderson tells us he is twenty-seven, and he is still in the bachelor state. He modestly says he is the champion golfer of the combination, and is a keen sportsman.

It was inevitable that someone would start up a Chick Henderson Fan Club. The young lady who set up the "Chick Henderson Friendship Circle" was Evelyne Arnold, who lived at 2 Lenthall Road, Dalston, London.E8. She was an "Astoria" addict, dancing to the Joe Loss Band at the Astoria Dance Salon with Chick's vocals, as many nights a week as she could afford. She and Chick were good friends, and Joe agreed to be the chairman of the Friendship Club, especially when he

Chick Henderson Friendship Circle

Secretary:
Evelyne Arnold,
2 Lenthall Road,
Dalston, E.8

Membership
Card

Chick (centre) clowning around as usual with members of the Joe Loss Band.

learned that Evelyne intended organising trips to and parties at the "Astoria". In fact, Joe autographed the reverse side of all of the membership cards and membership cost 10 pence a year – (two shillings in English currency of 1938). Over 2,000 fans joined the Club.

Commercial radio was reaching its zenith at that time. Banned in the U.K., commercial radio was heard only from the Continent, from stations like Radio Luxembourg and Radio Lyons. Aware of the big attraction of Joe Loss and Chick Henderson, Meltonian Shoe Dressing signed up the outfit to broadcast from Luxembourg and Normandy. Of course, no British artiste ever "broadcast" from those places. What they did was use either the Crystalate (later 'Decca') Studio, or the EMI Studio at St. John's Wood, to record the programmes on to totally inadequate 12" 78 rpm discs. To disguise, if not eliminate, the hiss of the discs, Crystalate used what they called "broadcast quality" shellac – a very fine powder base on to a paper laminate. EMI were to press on Vinylite, but not until 1942. In the 1930's they used a better quality shellac for "broadcasts". At the time of writing, none of these Loss/Henderson discs have been located, and it is possible that as only half a dozen were ever pressed off each one, none now exist. Because of this continental broadcasting, however, more fans were added to the C.H.F.C. (Chick Henderson Friendship Club). The musical press gave publicity to the Club and more members enrolled, until World War 2 stopped the entire project.

From bottom to top: Joe Loss, Chick Henderson, Monte Rey, Shirley Lenner (Blackpool 1939).

Chick began to feature in the "Melody Maker" poll, which sought to establish the Nation's favourite male/female dance band vocalists, leaders, and musicians. He had become a force to be reckoned with in the Music profession. Pam Stevenson however, told me that prior to visiting the "Astoria", she had never heard of Chick, although the name of Joe Loss was well known to her. Nevertheless, the musical press, and other branches of the media, often sought his opinions. For example, bandleader Felix Mendelssohn, who had a conventional line-up before forming his "Hawaiian Serenaders", decided to form a "Crooners' Protection Society".

The success of modern song stylists, or 'crooners', was phenomenal – and this angered the 'straight' singers, who had become quite peeved that their dated styles were becoming as popular as long-johns in a nudist camp! Abuse in the press, and even on the radio, was hurled at the 1930's pop stars, just like today. The "Sunday Pictorial" asked Chick Henderson what he thought about the Protection Society for Crooners, and he replied – "The crooner is always being kicked. It's time he kicked back. I know crooners who could sing straight singers off their feet!"

Just four years earlier, as if to prove the point, Al Bowlly recorded a baritone song, "Glorious Devon", on one side of a gramophone record, whilst a tenor named Owen Bryngwyn sang a pop song of the day on the other side.

It proved one thing – neither could sing successfully the 'other' type of song!

The aim of the "Crooners' Protection Society" was two fold:

1. To discourage abuse from a noisy minority of listeners.
2. To preserve their status – and their pay packets.

JOE LOSS AND AN 11 PIECE BAND

His 1939 personnel was Trumpets: Clem Stevens, Harry Letham, Stan Stanton; Trombones: Bill Burton, Bill Boland; Reeds: Reg Brewster, Eddie Pratt, Mickie Lewis, Danny Miller; Rhythm: Harry Kahn (Piano), Les Vinall (Guitar), Reg Richman (Bass), Jackie Greenwood (Drums).

SOLO RECORDING ARTISTE

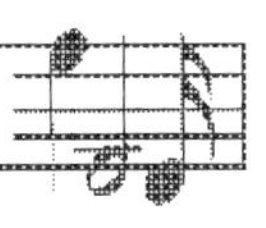

When a dance band vocalist achieved a certain degree of popularity, he stood a good chance of being asked to make a gramophone record. Chick was no exception. In May 1937, the company for whom the Joe Loss outfit (and Chick) recorded, Regal-Zonophone, asked if Chick Henderson would make a record of two songs of the day. They asked for – "The greatest mistake of my life", and Chick chose his particular favourite, "Broken-hearted clown". The recording took place on 20th July, 1937, and Regal provided the rather frugal backing of one accordeon and a piano. "Broken-hearted clown", especially with the accordeon, gives the impression that Chick is giving an impression of a "street" singer (of which there were many in the depressed days of the 1930's – they sang, often literally, for their bread and jam – butter being a luxury!). Chick recites part of the lyric in an "over the top" dramatic, almost hysterical fashion, which must surely have embarrassed him in later years, if not immediately he heard the playback. The record sold out its initial pressing and was followed by a better offer four months later on 20th November, when Joe Loss and his Band took second billing to Chick as they 'accompanied' him in a non-dance version of "Old Pal of Mine" and "After all these years" – arguably the best of all 1930's crooner solo records because of the full backing, good arrangements, colla vocé, as well as tempo and fine singing quality. The record was withdrawn (deleted} within a year and the 1939 catalogue printed in May listed only "Broken-hearted Clown" as being by Chick Henderson. Could it be that Joe Loss objected to taking second billing – so "Regal Zonophone" dropped it? Some people think so.

On 5th July, 1939, in that delightful hot, sunny summer, Chick recorded another "solo" – "Begin the Beguine". This time, Mr. Loss was not playing second billing. Despite the fact that, apart from a 2 bar rhythm only intro, the entire recording is by Chick Henderson, the record was catalogued as "Begin the Beguine" – Joe Loss and his

3 weeks after recording "Begin the Beguine" Chick took a holiday in Italy. He loved Italy. (August 1939)

Band, MR 3098. The thousands of record buyers who asked for Chick Henderson singing "Begin the Beguine" were told – "He hasn't recorded it!" Despite this lunatic decision, the recording went on to break all records, by being the only British record of the 1930's to sell a million. Finding the recording in the "Regal-Zonophone" catalogue was difficult and gave the impression that EMI didn't really care if it sold or not. No such recording as "Begin the Beguine" by Chick Henderson appeared in their general lists. However, under "Dance Records", the miniscule section did have an entry.

A more lunatic event was to follow. In December 1957, the recording was issued in Australia as a 45 rpm disc 45EA 4320 coupled with "Starlight Serenade" (OEA 9426). In 1939 it appeared in Holland on "Gloria" GZ 3275, together with its English coupling "My Prayer" (CAR 5471-1). In December 1939, it was issued in India on "TWIN" (FT 8755) with the same coupling. The Holland edition was deleted in May 1942 (during the war!) In February 1955 the record was DELETED in the U.K., along with the rest of the "Regal-Zonophone" catalogue – unbelievable but true! In 1963 it was re-issued in the U.K. on an Extended Play record, number 7EG 8875.

IN OCTOBER 1964 ENGLISH EMI DESTROYED THE MASTER!!!

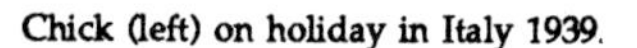

Chick (left) on holiday in Italy 1939.

Italy August 1939

HOW EMI LOST £1,000's

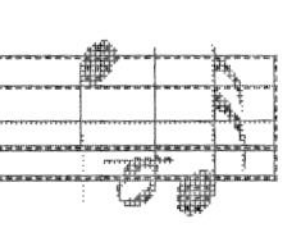

This is the Regal-Zonophone catalogue. There is no listing of the ballad by Chick Henderson of "Begin the Beguine".

REGAL

ZONOPHONE

In Alphabetical Order

Abanico (El), March (Grand Massed Bds.) MR749

ACCORDEON SERENADERS—
MR3771 { Cruising Down the River*. It's Been a Long Long Time*.

ADAMS, Capt. B.—*See* Salvation Army.

ALEXANDER'S ACCORDEONS—
MR1218 { Alice Blue Gown (from 'Irene')* Ramona.*
MR1635 { Because I Love You, Waltz*. I'm Forever Blowing Bubbles, Waltz*

Alice Blue Gown—*See* Irene.

Along the Navajo Trail (Roy Rogers) MR3807

Alpine Echoes (Foden's Band) MR3194

An Irish Lullaby (Jack Daly) MR2974

An Old Fashioned Tree (Gene Autry) MR3812

Answer to the Swiss Moonlight Lullaby (Montana Slim) MR3145

Apache Dance (Scott Wood Orchestra) MR1040

ASSURANCE SONGSTERS—*See* Salvation Army.

AUTRY, GENE (The Yodling Cowboy)—
MR2862 { Dust. The Old Trail. (Both with Instrumental accompaniment).
MR3404 { Blueberry Hill. Sierra Sue.
MR3455 { That Little Kid Sister of Mine. You Waited Too Long.
MR3477 { What's Gonna Happen to Me. Be Honest With Me.
MR3497 { El Rancho Grande (Give Me My Ranch) Little Old Band of Gold. (Both with Instrumental accompaniment).
MR3537 { Jail House Blues. Pistol Packin' Papa. (Both with Novelty accompaniment).
MR3588 { You Are My Sunshine. Mary Dear. (Both with Instrumental accompaniment).
MR3632 { I'll Never Let You Go (Little Darlin'). A Year Ago Tonight. (Both with Instrumental accompaniment).
MR3666 { Jingle, Jangle, Jingle. I'm a Cow Poke Pokin' Along. (Both with Instrumental accompaniment).
MR3728 { I'm Thinking Tonight of My Blue Eyes I'll be True While You're Gone.

AUTRY, GENE—*cont'd.*
MR3738 { When the Swallows Come Back to Capistrano. Darling, How Can You Forget So Soon.
MR3754 { Blue Hawaii. Paradise in the Moonlight.
MR3758 { Lonely River. I'll Wait For You. (Both with Instrumental accompaniment).
MR3782 { I Wish I Had Never Met Sunshine. You Only Want Me When You're Lonely (Both with String Band Accompaniment).
MR3809 { Silver Spurs. Someday you'll want me to want you
MR3812 { An old Fashioned tree. Here comes Santa Claus.
MR3814 { Boy from Texas—A Girl from Tennessee. Buttons and Bows.
MR3822 { Missouri Waltz Loaded Pistol and Loaded Dice.
MR3823 { Ole Faithful. I lost my little darlin'.
MR3824 { I'm a fool to care. A broken promise means a broken heart.

Ave Maria (*Bach-Gounod*) (Gracie Fields) MR1917

Away Out on the Mountain (Jimmie Rodgers) T5158

Bacio (Il) (Blue Hungarian Band) MR1273

Banjo Favourites (Raymonde Band o' Banjos) MR2774

Because (John McHugh) MR3470

Because I Love You, Waltz* (Alexander's Accordeons) MR1635

Be Honest With Me (Gene Autry) MR3477

BLACK DYKE MILLS BAND (Conducted by Arthur O. Pearce)—
MR3443 { Poem. Bless This House (Cornet Solo, W. A. Lang).

Blaze Away (Grand Massed Bands) MR1148

Bless 'Em All (No. 2) (George Formby) MR3441

Bless This House (Black Dyke Mills Bd.) MR3443

Bless This House (John McHugh) MR3470

In order to find "Begin the Beguine", a series called "Dance Records" had to be looked for.

In the 1951 catalogue, there were only seven "Dance" records. These included "Sans Cullottes" by American, Teddy Powell and his Swing Orchestra, and a foxtrot (Sic) by Joe Loss – "Begin the Beguine". The recording was also a bolero, according to small print on the label!!

The tiny asterisk * denoted there was a vocal on the disc. It never revealed the name of the singer who was, in fact, Chick Henderson.

DANCE RECORDS

At the Woodchoppers' Ball (S.T.) (Joe Loss) MR3243
Begin the Beguine, F.T.* (Joe Loss) MR3098
Bitin' the Dust, F.T. (Eric Winstone) MR3651
Conga, La (S.T.) (Joe Loss) MR2960
In an 18th Century Drawing Room, Q.S. (S.T.) (Joe Loss) MR3219
In Pine Top's Footsteps, F.T. (Teddy Powell) MR3598
In the Mood (S.T.) (Joe Loss) MR3243
My Prayer, S.F.T.* (Joe Loss) MR3098
Night Flight, F.T. (Eric Winstone) MR3651
Ode to Spring (Teddy Powell) MR3629
Palais Glide (S.T.) (Joe Loss) MR2706
Sans Culottes, F.T. (Teddy Powell) MR3598
So Deep is the Night, T. (S.T.) (Joe Loss) MR3219
Straight Eight Boogie, F.T. (Teddy Powell) MR3629

DANCING TIME FOR DANCERS SERIES

Played in Strict Tempo.

PLAYED BY JOE LOSS AND HIS BAND

At the Woodchoppers' Ball MR3243
In an 18th Century Drawing Room, Q.S. MR3219
In the Mood MR3243
Palais Glide MR2706
So Deep is the Night, T. MR3219

TO STRIP OR NOT TO STRIP?

It was inevitable that this most eligible of all the broadcasting and recording crooners would be a target for the most delectable cream of London "talent". One who made a fatal impression was a very pretty Show-biz artiste named "Jessica", who was a very graceful and talented dancer, who had appeared frequently in productions in cabaret in London, with another talented dancer named Bernard, and together they became Jessica-Bernard, performing at the Savoy, Kit Kat, Romano's and other top establishments of the day. One of the most successful of the Jessica-Bernard routines was the Bolero (Ravel), also called "The Seduction Dance" and, for this alone, they became extremely well known and popular in the West End. Bernard wanted Jessica to show even more of her beautiful talents. Prior to leaping into a mock volcano, he wanted to tear off her bra. There was no personal sex connotation here, and Bernard was reputedly a homosexual or "gay". Chick, however, exploded in true North of England indignation – "You are not going to appear topless, and that's that!" he said. "To strip or not to strip" became a burning issue. Here is how the press saw it. . . .

PAMELA HELEN STEPHENSON. She was part of a double act dancing duo. The moment she entered the Astoria Dance Salon where Chick worked, he fell in love with her.

As usual, the Press had got it all wrong.

The dancer's real name was Pamela Helen Stevenson. She was 19, and had formed a double act with Bernard. In order to improve their routines, she needed a good grounding in ballroom dancing. Whilst her parents would not permit her to visit such places as the Hammersmith Palais, or Locarno at Streatham, she was allowed to visit the Astoria which, at that time, attracted thousands of professional and amateur ballroom dancers. Indeed it was the best place of its kind.

TO strip or not to strip, that is the question. Dark-haired Jessica Stevens, half of the Jessica-Bernard act that does the famous "Seduction" dance in cabaret, is in a dilemma.

Should she appear in the nude? Employers say "Yes," but her boy-friend, Chick Henderson, the dance band vocalist, juts out his chin and says "No," firmly!

Jessica, swayed between love and art, is so far on the side of love. BUT IT'S COST HER THREE WEEKS' WORK!

LOVE AT FIRST SIGHT

One night Chick spotted Pam and sent a waitress over to her with a note which read – "Can I see you tonight after the Show? – Chick Henderson". She returned the piece of paper, on which she had written – "Sorry, I have a prior engagement!" – however, she added her telephone number. She had barely reached home when the 'phone rang. It was Chick! She accepted a 'date' with him and thus began a romance which culminated on the 30th April, the following year, 1940, at St. James' Church, Paddington, when they were married. The wedding certificate gives Chick's address "at the time of marriage" as 51 Raby Road, West Hartlepool. This was untrue, as he lived at 18 Northampton Avenue, Slough, in Buckinghamshire.

CHICK HENDERSON,
Vocalist.
Joe Loss & His Band.

18, Northampton Avenue,
Slough, Bucks.

THE WEDDING OF MR. HENDERSON ROWNTREE

Chick's hometown of Hartlepool gave his marriage scant attention in their local newspaper. Under the caption quoted above, the following thirteen lines only appeared:

WEDDING OF DANCE BAND VOCALIST

Many local people will be interested in the announcement of the wedding in London of Mr. Henderson Rowntree, son of Mr. and the late Mrs. Rowntree, of West Hartlepool, and Miss Pamela Helen Stevenson, of London. Mr. Rowntree is better known as Chick Henderson, vocalist with Joe Loss and his band. He is a native of Hartlepool, and has won a considerable reputation as a broadcaster and on the stage. As a boy he was a member of St. Hilda's Choir.

He gave his occupation as "Musician" which, of course, he was not! (When he joined the Royal Navy six months later on 8th October, 1940, he gave his occupation as "Variety Artist (Professional)". Pamela was described as "spinster" - no occupation, "aged 20".

Lynda Stevenson and Alex McBain were the witnesses - (her mother and Chick's best friend).

Wartime weddings were real forced economy affairs. To begin with, everything appeared to be rationed, or in short supply. To purchase a tie, cost one clothing coupon, a shirt six - and so on, but each individual person received only enough coupons to buy an outfit every year. Hiring was the order of the day, and new clothes were out. Wedding receptions had to be curtailed because food was rationed too. Finally, films for cameras were in still shorter supply and the taking of photographs was severely curtailed. One could be suspected of being a German spy if seen with a camera. No one was allowed to take pictures outside of factories, shipyards, Army, Air Force, or Naval establishments – or even barrage balloon sites. Honeymoons often had to wait until after the war!

Chick and Pamela had the Church wedding which they wanted and the Press photographs all featured a third party, Pamela's dog, David. The "Reception" was brief, for Chick had to dash off to rehearsals with the Joe Loss Band, which was appearing at a London Theatre that night. Neither Joe nor Mildred attended the wedding, though most of the Band did. The "honeymoon" was the rehearsal and the evening "performance" at the theatre.

After their wedding it was back to work for Chick, here the newly weds snatch an hour on the beach at Brighton

Towards the end of the Show, the crowd were clamouring for "Begin the Beguine" by Chick. This was the order of the day then. The "Beguine" was the final number. Chick sang the song and earned a standing ovation. When the cheering and applause died down, Joe Loss took the microphone and said – "Ladies and gentlemen, this is a very special and happy day for Chick Henderson, and it is my pleasure to tell you that he was married today!" The stunned silence was followed by howls of dismay and gasps of horror from the predominantly female audience. Momentarily thrown – Joe went back to the mike and said – "No, you mustn't wail and howl like that - - just wait until you see his pretty 20 year old bride – bring her on stage, Chick". Chick brought a shy and protesting Pamela on stage – then someone began to clap – then more joined in. This seemed to steady the boat a little – then Chick sang with the Band "Who's taking you home tonight?", with Pamela standing beside him.

CHICK AND JOE LOSS BUST UP

Having hit the jackpot with "Begin the Beguine" and been denied the credit for the runaway success of the record, Chick began to feel anger at the way he was being treated. Night after night the crowds demanded that he sang "Begin the Beguine". Then they would demand it again and again – One night he sang it three times. Undoubtedly it was *his* hit and not the Band's, and he was deeply hurt by the injustice. Joe Loss quite wrongly regarded the hit as his. Chick felt, also, that he deserved better remuneration – a view not shared by Joe Loss who, like other similar bandleaders, would pay up to a certain amount but no more. In their opinion, the No. 1 'star' was the leader. There were no other 'stars'. Indeed, one bandleader used to say – "and now *my* clarinet player will play". The leader 'owned' the lot and if anyone rocked the boat, they were free to go. Northerners stand on their feet . . . and their dignity! Chick left.

In 1973, Joe Loss told the writer that he felt Chick had been a bit "big-headed" over the "Beguine" recording. Those who knew Chick would deny this vehemently. In 1937, "Rhythm" magazine had said this:

"Mark my words, Chick Henderson crooner with Joe Loss's band, is gonna get to the very top. He's good, but the knowledge won't give Chick a swelled head."

(Three years later, readers' letters to the "Melody Maker" voted (1) Denny Dennis, (2) Chick Henderson, (3) Sam Browne, and (4) Al Bowlly, as the Nation's favourites).

Chick felt so strongly about the subject of Joe Loss that he caused a sensation by quitting the Joe Loss Organisation. He made front page news in the "Melody Maker". Whoever wrote the piece did a very clumsy cover-up. The caption read:

"CHICK HENDERSON LEAVES LOSS"

The sub-title was "NATIONAL SERVICE DEPLETES BAND", and the first paragraph doesn't mention Chick at all. The second paragraph refers to Joe Loss's appearance at the Alhambra Theatre, Bradford, and says, "Last week at the Winter Gardens, Morecambe, was a memorable occasion insofar as it was the final appearance with the Band of Chick Henderson". He went on to say that Chick had left to "undertake work of National importance!" Later it suggested that he had gone to work in a munitions factory!!

In reality, he had signed up with Harry Roy and began immediately to be featured at the Café Anglais where Harry Roy was in residency. He remained with Harry until he was called up, broadcasting, and recording, as well as wowing the wealthy at this plush nightspot. The "Melody Maker" reporter,

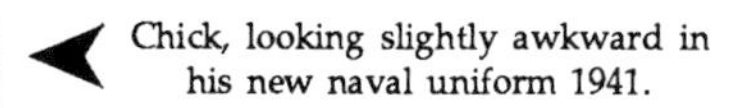

Chick, looking slightly awkward in his new naval uniform 1941.

H.M. KING GEORGE VI
inspects the sailors.
(Did he realise that Chick Henderson was 5th from the left in the back row).

CHICK JOINS THE NAVY
(second from the right - back row).

obviously aware of the real reasons behind Chick's bustup with Joe Loss, goes on to say in a very snide tone . . . "In the case of Chick Henderson, however, it would appear that big as Joe's loss (no pun here) may seem on the surface, it is surely completely minimised by the terrific success achieved on his opening on Monday last by his successor – a seventeen year old London boy, Bob Arden, who Joe had kept up his sleeve for a long time, in anticipation of such an emergency.

When Chick Henderson first went to Joe Loss, he went as a completely unknown provincial vocalist, and he would probably be the first to admit that the backing and assistance he has derived from Joe and the band have helped more than a little in developing his latent talent and placing him in the forefront of dance band vocalists in this country."

Harry Roy gave Chick more freedom than Joe Loss, and the pair of them enjoyed, with great relish, Chick singing and broadcasting "Begin the Beguine" – acccompanied by Harry Roy's fabulous wartime band.

Joe Loss, who claimed the song was *his* hit, had to be content with Harry Kaye singing it for him, until finally, he simply copied the Artie Shaw instrumental version with a clarinet lead.

Joining Harry Roy in June 1940, Chick had already considered his future role in the War. He was certain he would not be called up to Active Service because he had very bad varicose veins. It was true that he had possibly envisaged himself in an "exempt" occupation on essential war work in a munitions factory, but at his "Medical" in May of 1940, doctors were prepared to consider him because of his Marine Engineering background, as an Engine Room Artificer in the Royal Navy.

It suited him to stay with Harry Roy until his country made its mind up. This Britain did, when, on 8th October, 1940, he was given the number C/MX 73092.

If a copy of this Form is required, Form S. 1243 is to be used.

S.—459 (Revised—August, 1939).

A

5/1

Cut along here.

CERTIFICATE of the Service of

SURNAME. (In Block Letters)	CHRISTIAN NAME OR NAMES.
ROWNTREE	Henderson

in the Royal Navy.

NOTE.—The corner of this Certificate is to be cut off where indicated if the man is discharged with a "Bad" character or with disgrace, or if specially directed by the Admiralty. If the corner is cut off, the fact is to be noted in the Ledger.

Port Division: Chatham

Official No.: C/MX 73092

Man's Signature on discharge to Pension

Date of Birth: 22nd November 1912

Nearest known Relative or Friend. (To be noted in pencil.)

Relationship: Wife

Name: Pamela Helen

Where { Town or Village: Hartlepool

Section of Chick's Naval papers.

SOMEWHERE AT SEA

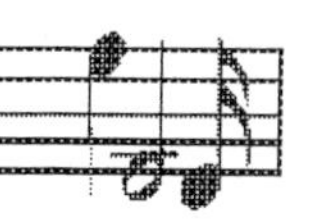

The official Royal Navy records of the War, state where Chick spent his war service:

The 19th March, 1943 to 24th December, 1943 is listed as "Canada".

(The purpose of this long visit is not given on his official papers, but it was to pick up a special submarine being built there and to return it to England).

On the 12th June, 1944, he was promoted to Sub-Lieutenant. One of his 'Chiefs' remembers him well – "Buster" Brown, who today is "J. C. Brown", Engineer, ex Royal Navy and Admiralty Boiler Examiners Tester.

"When I was serving as a Chief Engineroom Artificer (C.E.R.A.) on the Cruiser H.M.S. London, 1941-42, Chick Henderson was drafted to us as E.R.A. Henderson Rowntree. He was a most unpretentious chap, a good workman and a popular mess-mate with a great sense of humour. At the time his most popular record was of "Begin the Beguine" which was often played over our T.S.F. We'd persuade him to sing to it and he'd oblige. He told us he had difficulty in reaching the final, very high note, and to achieve it he would jump up onto a chair and haul his trousers up tight – to tremendous applause!

Returning from leave, on which he had appeared with Joe Loss and his Band, he told us he'd been approached by Lady Jellicoe, who wanted him to sing at one of her concerts a few weeks later. On being told that, unfortunately, he would then be at sea, she remarked – "What a pity, I'm sure that if Jellicoe were alive he would have arranged for you to come!" He laughed when he said to us – "You can just imagine the Commander in Chief putting himself out for a blinking crooning Tiffy!"

I was doing a bit of photography at the time and I remember copying a photo of his wife and child and tinting it for him.

I was sad to hear of his death. A real nice chap.

Sincerely, J. C. (Buster) Brown.

Someone who met him at the Dockyard at Chatham was a "Geordie" from Gateshead, Bob Pace.

He takes up the story . . .

"I first met Chick when he was called up for the Royal Navy, in October, 1940. I met him in the Dockyard when he was doing his training to be a Dockyard Artificer. He was quite a good fitter, by the way – a great fitter. He and I chummed up, being North-Easterners. I don't know why, but we just seemed to get on together. We were very friendly. Where I went, he went – and, after a while, he used to take me up to London to meet his friends and his wife. That is when he went to live at 27 Tring Avenue, Ealing. That was his last home address, to my knowledge.

Anyhow, in April 1940, he was drafted to a ship which was lying at Freetown, Sierra Leone. I volunteered to go with him because he was my 'oppo'. We joined our Merchant Cruiser, called the "Comorin", at Greenock on the Saturday morning before Palm Sunday. We sailed in the forenoon and the following day, on the Palm Sunday morning, it was really rough, blowing about a Force 8 gale. There were two destroyers in the convoy, escorting H.M.S. "Lincoln". Incidentally the First Lieutenant of H.M.S. "Broke" was Peter Scott, the naturalist.

The first survivors, Chick amongst them are pulled to the rescue ship.

The first boat of survivors leaves the stricken ship Chick is amongst them.

On the Sunday afternoon I was lying on my bunk. Chick came to me and says - - "Bob", he says, "the boat's on fire!" I believe it was a blowback in one of the boilers, and the boat was on fire. Couldn't do anything with it. There's nothing worse than a fire at sea – you just cannot control it, especially in that wind.

So – we went up on deck. We had to throw ammunition over the side in case it went off. Then, about 8 o'clock in the evening, the Captain ordered "Abandon Ship – All non-swimmers first". Chick, poor Chick, couldn't swim, so I helped him over the side. I got him down the poles and I put him into a lifeboat, and I climbed back on board because I could swim. I watched him getting picked up in the distance by the "Lincoln". I thought – "Well, he's made it. I can make it". I went over the side. I didn't get picked up until the following forenoon. I was lucky enough to get picked up by the "Lincoln" and they carried me down to the boiler room.

Incidentally, the man who picked me out of the water so happened to be a friend of mine who lived in Gateshead – a lad called Freddy Cowan of Ford Street, Bensham. I thought he was going to throw me back, to tell the truth!

Anyhow, they put me in the boiler room and Chick was there. He looked after me, because I couldn't do much. We sailed back to Greenock. We were very lucky incidentally, because the remaining survivors were picked up and taken to Freetown!

When we got to Greenock, we took a train up to Glasgow Central Station. Chick says to me – "I wonder how long we've got to wait, Bob, before we can get back to Chatham?". It turned out we had three hours to wait for the train. Incidentally, that night Harry Roy was playing Green's Playhouse, so Chick and I got permission and the two of us went up there. They made us most welcome. Harry Roy's brother was there, and Marjorie Kingsley who was, I believe, singing with the band at that time. We had a good night – a really good evening. It took the edge off the troubles we had been through.

Never mind – we found our way back to Chatham eventually and we got our survivors' leave. I managed to go up and see Chick at the Astoria, and we had some good evenings.

Then I went with him to a couple of recording sessions with Joe Loss and his Band for HMV. The two records he made were "Dolores" and "Sand in my Shoes". They were made in the Kingsway Hall in London, in September, 1941, and Chick had just returned to Joe after the breakup, for recording purposes and broadcasts. He made these records at 7.30 a.m. on a Sunday morning! We didn't get to bed, incidentally, till 4 o'clock that same morning!

APRIL 1941 - H.M.S. COMORIN TAKES FIRE. NON SWIMMERS TAKE TO THE FIRST BOAT (Pictured) CHICK IS ABOARD THIS CRAFT.
(Picture taken by First Lieutenant of rescue ship Peter Scott - later famous naturalist).

Anyway – on the Sunday afternoon I met Joe Loss and Chick, and he introduced me to them all. I managed to meet the tenor sax in the band at the time. They called him "Limerick". He was from Limerick. Norman Impey was his name. We went to the London Jazz Jambouree at the London Palladium that afternoon and we had a real 'humdinger' of a time . . . thoroughly enjoyed ourselves.

When we got back to Chatham, I thought to myself . . . "Bob, I've had enough of these surface craft", and I volunteered for the Submarine Service. Chick? – he called me worse than . . . you know! Eventually, he got a draft to H.M.S. "London", a cruiser. And the last time I saw Chick – I came down from Scotland, for I knew the boat was in dry dock at Hebburn. I went down to see him. We went to the Oxford Galleries that night. I think Peter Fielding was still playing with his Band, and Chick got up and sang a song – and that was it! Everybody used to shout for the same old faithful, "Begin the Beguine" but he had a lot more favourites than that – to my knowledge anyhow. There was one in particular. I was in a nightclub with him one night, in Rupert Street, Soho. The "Penthouse", they called it. Chick and I, and his wife, Pam. He got up and sang "Smoke gets in your Eyes" – and I don't think he ever recorded it, but I believe it was one of his favourites.

He was Britain's No. 1 crooner, apparently, then he had to join the Navy. I knocked around with him and I didn't even know who he was. As far as I was concerned, he was another "Geordie". When I discovered his true identity, it is true to say, he never let the fact go to his head that he was Britain's most popular male singer."

From Bob Pace's account, Chick appears to have buried the hatchet as far as Joe Loss was concerned, because he returned to the recording studios of EMI with Joe to make subsequent records when he was home on leave during 1941-42 (see discography). He did not record with any other groups after that.

MOBILE RECORDING

Joe Loss toured during the war and the worst of the blitzes. He recorded via the EMI mobile recording unit, which visited Coventry (hit even worse than London in one night), Weston-Super-Mare, Blackpool, Bristol, Leeds, Glasgow (where Chick had caught him for his last session), Bradford, Dudley, Liverpool, Birmingham, Southport, Manchester, Ardwick, Wolverhampton, and even Newcastle upon Tyne (whose natural dance band talent had only once been given a chance to record, and that was in 1929).

Joe Loss broadcast from many of these places.

Jerry Dawson of the "Melody Maker's" Northern notes recalled:

"I dropped in on a Joe Loss broadcast and, amongst many things, was particularly struck with Harry Kaye's singing of the current hit "Amor, Amor". On this performance Harry is surely our most underrated vocalist, although he is always a hit in the Loss stage show.

In the current offering, which I heard at Ilford, I saw and heard the show from the wings, having failed to get into the theatre by ordinary means, so packed was the house. Harry has the unenviable job of singing the vocal to "Begin the Beguine" – a spot which all Loss fans will automatically associate with the late and never-to-be-forgotten Chick Henderson."

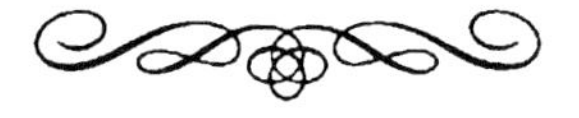

2

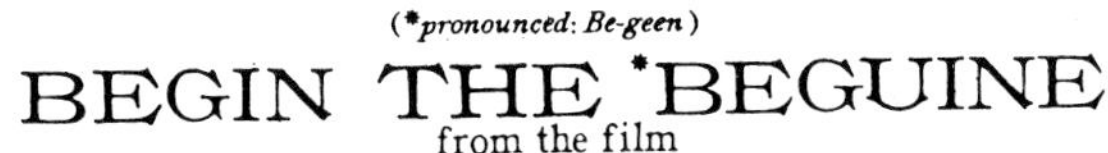

Words and Music by COLE PORTER

CHICK'S ONLY CHILD IS BORN

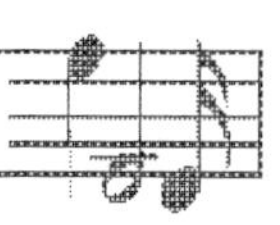

Chick was home on leave when his only child, Lynda Ann, was born on July 5th, 1941.

His wife, Pamela, takes up the story . . .

"Previous to the birth, Chick had become an eagerly awaited visitor at the Maternity Ward. The Matron, who was a bit of a battleaxe and feared by the staff, had a different approach towards Chick. She was totally captivated by him. Eventually, the baby was born. Chick, by his omnipresence at the ward, saw the baby before her mother. He was so exuberant (although he was expecting a son), that he slid down the bannister straight into the Matron's office, clutching a bottle of Navy Rum. "Yippee", he cried, as he handed over the bottle of 100% proof Navy Rum. He and the Matron drank a toast. He spent over an hour with her, laughing, chatting and joking, and it is true to say that she had not been seen to be so happy before. The baby was baptised Lynda Ann some two weeks later, and one of Chick's sisters Mary Elizabeth made the journey to be present as godmother."

Lynda Ann Rowntree is christened at the Parish Church.

This was to be their only child. Today, Lynda Ann lives in Hampshire. She was only 2½ years old when her father died and she has no conscious recollection of him, but her mother, Pamela, ensured that the little girl was brought up to know who her father was, and all the evidence of his artistry was given to her. All through the years to the present time, Lynda has cherished the 78 rpm discs that remain of her father, including test pressings with Harry Roy and his Band, and a little snapshot album, together with his Certificate of Service in the Royal Navy.

She presented the 78 rpm discs to me when I visited her in Hampshire in mid 1990. She collected re-issue LP's that she came across in record shops, even if there was only one track included of her father's singing.

When asked how she felt her father rated compared to the other crooners of the day, she replied that she had never listened to them. She was only interested in the voice of her father. This, I suppose, is understandable. Music of the 40's, the decade in which she was born, could have little interest to her in the 1990's, except when she could have that rare opportunity of hearing her father's voice. During her school days, she talked frequently to her chums about her father. His voice was well known to many of the children and to all of the staff, as his recording of "Begin the Beguine" was played regularly on the radio, just as it has continued to be played in the 1990's.

Chick's only child, daughter Lynda Ann, aged 2½

She told me that no-one has ever interviewed her or her mother regarding her Dad, and this one fact alone makes the story very sad because when the "Daily Mirror" mentioned the fact that I was hoping to launch the Chick Henderson Appreciation Society, over 200 letters and telephone calls were received, and, as these words are written, I have just spoken to a group of jazz musicians playing in the "Porthole" at North Shields, and among them was Denny Boyce, the former bandleader. Their thoughts collectively were expressed by Hughie Aitchison, the veteran trumpet player from Tyneside, who said – "It is about time that such a Society was formed. It can never be too late" – so let's hope it gets under way quickly.

In a letter to shipmate Bob Pace, Chick describes his darling little girl:

➡

Pamela is well, and the baby is getting bigger & bigger. She has sprouted a couple of teeth, which enhance her beauty. Altogether, she is a great baby — perfectly formed bodily — and a face which is beautifully moulded and is so intelligent, that she looks like a beautiful woman in miniature. I cannot keep but compare her expression with the inevitable inane apathetic look of most other babies. She will have progressed a lot, before I see her again. She will perhaps greet me on the station.

Hey what sort of a job have you got. When I look at your address, I can't help thinking that you have an easy number. You lucky old so-and-so!

Well so long pal, give my best to your wife

All the best

Chick

In a letter to shipmate Bob Pace, Chick describes his darling little girl.

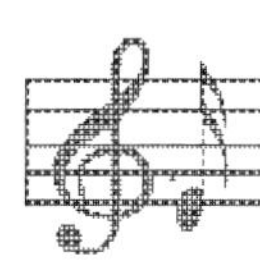

CANADA — THEN PROMOTION

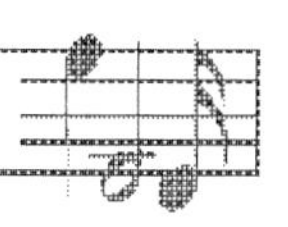

In the U.K., Servicemen were officially described as being "Somewhere in France" or "Somewhere at Sea". Chick was officially "Somewhere at Sea", but after arriving in Canada in March 1943, it became obvious that the stay in Canada was going to be a long one - if not a boring one - so Chick decided to offer his Services to the Canadian Broadcasting Company. "Chick who?" they asked him. He was quite hurt that no one appeared to have heard of him or his recordings and broadcasts. He was incensed when asked to attend for an audition to see if he was good enough to be considered. It is to his credit that he acquiesced, and soon the "Singing Sailor", as they dubbed him, got his first broadcast. A lot of mail was received as a result and, within a very short time, Chick found himself with two radio series. Radio CBY and CBL featured him. On CBY he appeared in a series with Russ Jerow and his Orchestra. The show was called "Reminiscing", and was broadcast on Thursdays at 8.05 p.m. On CBL he appeared with two pianists every Saturday at 7.15 p.m. The shows showed up well in the 'ratings' but, unfortunately, no commercial recordings were made and no 'on air' recordings or 'off air' recordings appear to have been made.

Chick in Canada

He returned to Chatham on Christmas Day 1943, and on 18th April he was back with H.M.S. "Victory". On 7th May, 1944, he was again with H.MS. "Pembroke".

The last entry in his "Certificate of Service" reads . . .

12th June, 1944:
Promoted to Sub-Lieutenant

Right through the war, he maintained letter contact with his roots – his many relations in Hartlepool.

It was a jubilant Chick who wrote to his youngest sister, Freda, from the Royal Naval Barracks at Chatham in 1944.

H. ROWNTREE E.R.A.,
C/MX 73092.
ICE. MESS.
R.N. BARRACKS
CHATHAM.

Saturday.

Dear Freda

In response to yours.

I shall be on the air on Thursday in "Navy Mixture". I believe it comes on about 6.15.

I have finished my course and have successfully passed the examination & am now waiting to go on leave. It is usual to give leave, to get the new uniforms, and that is what I'm impatiently awaiting. Then I shall be a real Sub. Lieut. — yoicks!

I am actually home on week end leave now and as I have to write to Mary and Sam is going to give me a manicure, I'll hop off

Love to all

Chick.

TRAGEDY

Right then he was at the Royal Naval Barracks at Southsea in the Mess Annexe at the Royal Pier Hotel, which had been requisitioned by the Admiralty. At that time, the Nazis were sending over "flying" bombers, although these were literally flying bombs. They were pilotless planes, timed fuel-wise to reach a particular area – first London, then later, Portsmouth. Once the fuel was cut off, the droning of the planes ceased and they plummeted to the ground, exploding, destroying and killing. On Sunday evening, 25th June, 1944, the air raid warning sounded once again, and the British Ack-Ack gunners began firing at a flying bomb which was approaching Southsea. Chick, the Chaplain, and fellow officers decided to make their way to the nearest air raid shelter. They came down the emergency stairs at the rear of the hotel and began walking along the short outside path which led to the shelter.

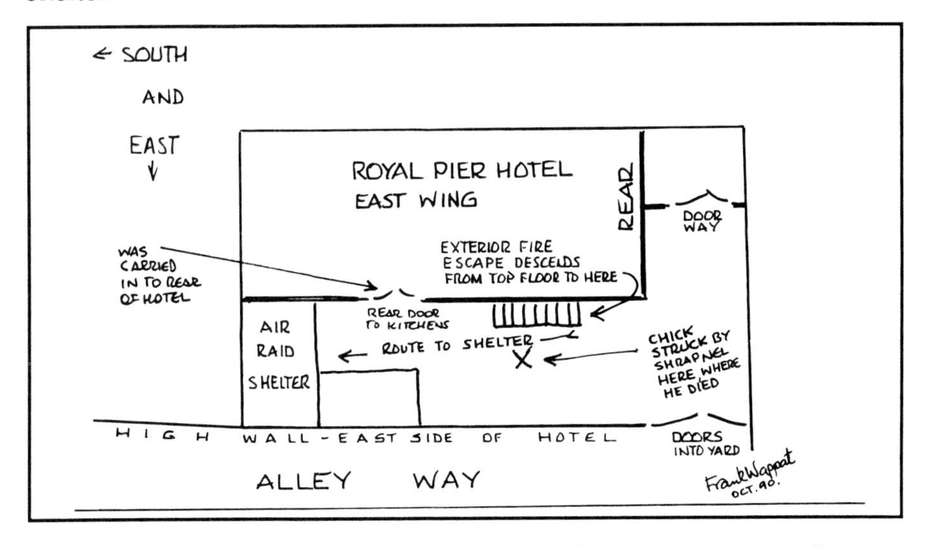

The Chaplain, Rev. C. B. Naylor, R.N.V.R. takes up the story in a letter to Chick's wife the very next day.

Monday, 26th June, 1944.

Dear Mrs. Rowntree,

This may be the first letter that you open bringing you the very sad news of the fatal accident that occurred to your husband last night here at Southsea. It is with very great regret that I write to tell you about this.

We were all making our way to the shelters after a warning – we could distinctly hear the pilotless 'plane in the sky. "Chick", as his friends all called him, was in the passageway leading from the emergency stairs to the shelter, when he was suddenly seen to fall unconscious. We carried him into the back of the hotel where it was warm, and sent for the doctor. "Chick" did not regain consciousness. A splinter from an exploded shell or metal container had pierced his side. It was a quick and painless death. I can assure you he had very little pain or physical suffering.

We are all deeply distressed at this terrible accident, and I know I am speaking on behalf of all the Officers here when I say how much we sympathise with you in your sorrow. "Chick" was very popular here, and liked by everyone. I have had long chats with his cabin-mates and friends, and they have told me how devoted he was to you and to his little daughter. He was a splendid fellow, and one we can ill do without these days.

This must be a terrible time for you, and I feel deeply for you in your sorrow. When I lost my own father very recently, the one thought that kept me firm was the confident belief that he is still living in a new experience, a new life, call it what you will. I do beg you to be fully assured that our friend whom we call "Chick" is still living in a world we cannot at present see, but which we shall in time come to see, and where we shall meet again those who have passed on. Believe that he still cares for you, as you still care for him, and that if you are confident in your mind about this, he will be happy and better able to carry out the new work that lies before him. Believing this, and confident that this is the truth, and praying to the Father of us all to strengthen him and you, you will find, I know, that the bonds that linked you together become in a very wonderful way firmer and stronger than ever before. You and your little daughter will be remembered in my prayers tonight and I shall also pray for "Chick" that God will give him strength in his new work in that Unseen World.

Please believe me to be sincere in all that I write, and accept this small message of deep sympathy.

Yours very sincerely,
C. B. Naylor.

The Hartlepool edition of the "Daily Mail" paid a lamentably short tribute.

Death of Chick Henderson

The many friends of Sub-Lt. Henderson Rowntree will learn with regret of his death on active service. Sub-Lt. Rowntree was called to the Royal Navy just over 3½ years ago. Better known as Chick Henderson, dance band vocalist, he had appeared with various well-known combinations, such as Harry Leader's, Joe Loss's, and Harry Roy's. Aged 31, he leaves a widow and a daughter aged three years, now residing at Ealing.

Sub-Lt. Rowntree was formerly a member of St. Hilda's choir, and a memorial service will be held for him to-morrow evening.

A larger space was taken up the following year by Chick's relatives as they remembered him in the "In Memorium" column.

IL. MONDAY, JUNE 25, 1945

ROWNTREE. — Sub./Lieut. (E.) H. Rowntree, R.N.V.R. To the most precious memory of my beloved husband and Lynda's daddy, who lost his life on active service one year ago to-day. — Pamela Helen Rowntree.

ROWNTREE.—A token of remembrance of my dearly beloved brother, Henderson, who was killed on active service, June 25, 1944.—Never forgotten by his loving sister Nan, Walter, and family.—Some day we'll understand.

ROWNTREE.—Treasured memories of my darling brother, Henderson, Sub.-Lieut., R.N.V.R., killed on active service, June 25, 1944.—For ever in the thoughts of his loving sister Freda and brother-in-law Norman.—Longing for you daily.

ROWNTREE.—Sweet memories of my dear brother, Henderson, Sub-Lieut., R.N.V.R., killed on active service, June 25, 1944.—Longed for always by his loving sister Hilda.—Always a beautiful memory.

ROWNTREE. — Sub./Lieut. (E.) H. Rowntree, R.N.V.R. A token of love and remembrance of my dear brother (Chick Henderson), killed on active service, June 25, 1944.—His memory to me is a treasure, his loss a lifelong regret.—Mary, Norman, Jean, and Keith.

ROWNTREE.—Henderson, Sub.-Lt.: R.N.—A token of love and remembrance to our dear brother, killed on active service one year ago.—Always in the thoughts of his sisters Eva and Ethel, brothers-in-law, and nephews.—His duty nobly done.

ROWNTREE.—In proud memory of my brother, Sub.-Lieut. Henderson Rowntree, R.N.V.R., killed on active service: June 25, 1944.—Dick.

ROWNTREE.—Loving memories of my dear brother, Henderson, died June 22, 1944.—Always remembered by Bob, Mary and family.

HOW THE MEDIA SAW IT

Although Chick was killed on Sunday evening, the news was not released until later on Monday – too late for more than a brief mention in the "Melody Maker" which 'went to bed' on Tuesdays. However, the following Thursday, the tragedy shared front page billing with the news that Harry Roy was opening at his own new "Milroy" Club, which was at 41-44 Stratton Street, Mayfair.

Under the caption, "Death of Chick Henderson", plus a picture of the Sub-Lieutenant, the "Melody Maker" said:

"Once again the war has hit the entertainment profession and cut short the career of yet another young celebrity.

This time, (as briefly announced last week), it is our very sad duty to record the passing of famous ex-Joe Loss vocalist, Chick Henderson, (Sub-Lieutenant Henderson Rowntree, R.N.), whose tragic death, whilst on active service, occurred last week. The interment took place at Portsmouth last Thursday, 28th.

Chick Henderson who was born in South Shields, and was in his early thirties, occupied a unique position in the musical world, built up largely through his long association with Joe Loss, with whose band he appeared for over nine years.

Not only was Chick one of the finest and most popular of all the battery of vocalists who have appeared with the Loss Band up and down the country, but through his records and broadcasts he made friends and admirers all over the world.

Quite recently, as a star featured artist, he had carried out a series of exceptionally successful solo broadcasts on the Canadian networks.

Chick, who was a qualified marine engineer, left Loss to join the Navy in 1941. Zealous attention to his duties had resulted in his promotion to Sub-Lieutenant shortly before his tragic death.

EXTENSIVE TRAVELS

During the course of his Naval duties, he travelled all over the world – went to South Africa, Russia and Canada, among many other places – and it was whilst ashore on special duties in Canada for a short time that he was able to carry out the broadcasts referred to above.

It is ironical indeed that Chick Henderson should have survived two terrible occasions when his ship was torpedoed on the high seas, only to meet his death so much nearer home.

Chick Henderson did one thing in his career that few singers have ever done before – he built a world-wide reputation literally on his performance of one song.

Those who have studied his career with Joe Loss's Band will need no telling that the song was "Begin the Beguine", and Chick's record of it is still one of the best-selling British records in recent years.

He will always be associated with this lovely song.

Joe Loss said to the "Melody Maker" – "In the tragic death of Chick Henderson, the profession loses a really great artist, and I lose a personal friend whose talents and whose companionship I shall never forget. He was not only a grand and conscientious singer, but a man of great personal charm and gentlemanliness. We shall always mourn him deeply; this goes for me, for Mrs. Loss, for the boys still left in my Band who had the pleasure of working with Chick; and for Miss Roxburgh, stage manager, Bill Tracy, and all members of my staff, who will always remember him."

Chick leaves a wife and baby daughter, to whom we join with the whole profession and with his friends all over the world in expressing our very deepest sympathy."

NOTE: The "Melody Maker" misprinted the date. It should have read Thursday, 29th June and not 28th – nor was he born in South Shields. He did not leave Loss in 1941.

The funeral, in fact, was not at Portsmouth at

all. The burial took palce in the Royal Naval Cemetery, Clayhall Road, Gosport, in the section set aside for Officers.

After his accidental killing, his body was taken to the Royal Naval Hospital, Gosport, where a post mortem was carried out.

CHICK'S WIFE - NUMB!

Pamela, his wife, had been notified by telegram of his death, and she recalled:

"I read the telegram . . . and read it, and read it again. I couldn't believe it! There must have been a mistake. I was just coming to terms with the fact that the war would soon be ended. The air raids had become fewer. We felt safer than before. I was living with my mother and baby daughter, and Chick was spending more time ashore, studying, learning. Enemy action at sea had been severely curtailed by the victorious Allies, and, at this time Chick was at the Royal Pier Hotel, Southsea, so how could they send a telegram saying he had been killed? No, I felt – there was definitely a mistake. I was numb. My mother tried to console me. I was totally confused. Telephone calls were made. Information was hard to come by. No-one seemed to know exactly what had happened, or if the telegram was in fact correct.

Chick was ashore. No one had been killed in the air raid of the previous day and no-one seemed to be in a different frame of mind to the one in which I found myself - - confused. The fact that it was Sunday made it more difficult for communication.

The next morning I received a letter from the Padre or Chaplain. He and Chick were friendly, and Chick himself always made a point of going to Church services. In fact, I remember photographing him coming out of Church with Sandy McPherson, the broadcasting organist. I took this photograph quite deliberately, because Chick had just lit a cigarette and was walking out of the Church gate with his friends, with the cigarette stuck between his lips. He looked an absolute 'yob' – but he enjoyed smoking his "Craven A".

Back to the telegram and his death, however . . .

As the reality of the situation dawned upon me, I became filled with anger. The anger was probably the outcome of the initial shock. He had survived two escapes at sea, one when his ship took fire and sank, and the other when his ship was torpedoed. He had braved the attacks and the threat of the Nazi 'U' boats as he sailed the seven seas. He, and his fellow men, had faced air attacks, the concealed mines in the sea, and now he had returned to England only to be killed by the British. It was the irony of the situation that it was not a German but a British shell, fired at a precise split second, which killed him, in a billion to one chance. In the space of a few seconds walk to the air raid shelter, a piece of British made shrapnel pierced his chest and his side, killing him instantly.

Grief, numbness, anger, confusion . . . I was 24, a widow, and my little girl had not yet reached her third birthday.

As everyone began to look forward to the final end of the war, peace at last, and a new world – mine appeared to have been destroyed with one piece of paper – the telegram!"

From:

Rev. C.B.Naylor: R.N.V.R.,
ROYAL NAVAL BARRACKS,
(Ward Room Mess Annexe)
ROYAL PIER HOTEL,
SOUTHSEA.

June 26th 1944.

Dear Mrs. Rowntree,

This may be the first letter that you open bringing you the very sad news of the fatal accident that occured to your husband last night here at Southsea. It is with very great regret that I write to tell you about this.

We were all making our way to the shelters after a warning - we could distinctly hear the pilotless 'plane in the sky. "Chick" - as his friends all called him - was in the passage-way leading from the emergency stairs to the shelter when he was suddenly seen to fall unconcious. We carried him into the back of the Hotel where it was warm, and sent for the Doctor. "Chick did not regain conciousness. A splinter from an exploded shell or metal container had pierced his side. It was a quick and painless death. I can assure you he had very little pain or physical suffering.

We are all deeply distressed at this terrible accident, and I know I am speaking on behalf of all the Officers here when I say how much we sympathise with you in your sorrow. "Chick" was very popular here, and liked by everyone. I have had long chats with his cabin-mates and friends, and they have told me how devoted he was to you and to his little daughter. He was a splendid fellow, and one we can ill do without these days.

This must be a terrible time for you, and I feel deeply for you in your sorrow. When I lost my own Father very recently, the one thought that kept me firm was the confident belief that he is still living in a new experience, a new life, call it what you will. I do beg you to be fully assured that our friend whom we called "Chick" is <u>still</u> living in a world we cannot at present see, but which we shall all in time come to see, and where we shall meet again those who have passed on. Believe that he still cares for you, as you still care for him, and that if you are confident in your mind about this, he will be happy and better able to carry out the new work that lies before him. Believing this, and confident that this is the truth, and praying to the Father of us all to strengthen him and you, you will find, I know, that the bonds that linked you together become in a very wonderful way firmer and stronger than ever before. You and your little daughter will be remembered in my prayers tonight and I shall also pray for "Chick" that God will give him strength in his new work in that Unseen World.

Please believe me to be sincere in all that I write; and accept this small message of deep sympathy.

Yours very sincerely,

C.B. Naylor.

C.B.NAYLOR.

LETTER FROM THE ADMIRALTY INFORMING OF CHICK'S DEATH

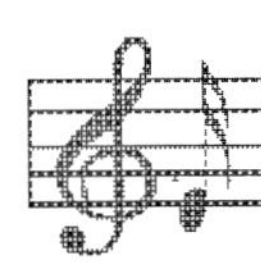

THE MYSTERY OF CHICK'S DEATH

The telegram telling of Chick's death on "Active Service" was sent on Monday, 26th June, to his widow, Pamela – the day after his death. Strictly speaking, the "Active Service" bit was not true, and gave the impression, quite wrongly, that he was killed *by* enemy action, whilst *fighting* the enemy. This is what the term "Active" denotes when used in this context.

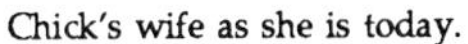

Chick's wife as she is today.

Chick's daughter as she is today.

That same day, the Chaplain wrote the letter to Pamela in which he clearly states "*We* (that is Chick, the Chaplain and others) were *all* making our way to the shelters after a warning", (i.e. an air raid warning siren being sounded at 11.00 p.m. on the Sunday evening).

"Chick . . . was in the passage way leading from the emergency stairs to the shelter when he was suddenly *seen* to fall unconscious. *We* carried him into the back of the hotel . . . "

At that early stage, the Chaplain states clearly, "a splinter from an exploded shell, or metal container, had pierced his side". Anyone else would have referred to the "splinter" as *shrapnel*. The word *splinter* indicates that this is his own eye-witness account (not an official Admiralty version), and adds more weight to his account, in comparison with the other two.

The mystery begins when the Surgeon, Commander Teasy, told Chick's widow that "Chick had gone out to post a letter and never returned". She confirmed that she did, in fact, receive a letter from Chick the day after he was killed. Later, Pamela sent a copy of the Chaplain's letter to the family in Hartlepool. She told them what the Surgeon Commander had told her. The family were puzzled by the two different accounts, and the "killed on Active Service" bit.

For over a year, Chick's widow and the family remained dis-satisfied, and eventually she wrote to the Admiralty regarding the matter. Compensation (he was killed by *British* shrapnel), widows' pensions, damages, liability – all kinds of thoughts spring to mind, not to mention the two conflicting stories.

COPY/JC 13th November, 1945.

NAVAL OFFICERS RELATIVES INFORMATION BUREAU.

Admiralty,
Queen Anne's Mansions,
St. James' Park,
S.W.1.

No. 4069 23rd October, 1945.

Dear Madam,

Thank you for your letter of the 22nd October.

I have seen the report of your husband's death, and this states that during the air raid at 11 p.m. on Sunday, 25th June, he was killed by a splinter. He was found in a state of collapse under the fire escape of the block of flats adjacent to the Pier Hotel, Southsea. The Pier Hotel First Aid Party was summoned and rendered immediate assistance, and a Medical Officer and ambulance were sent from the R.N. Barracks, but your husband passed away before the Medical Officer could get to him.

It is not certain how this came about, but your husband was probably struck by a splinter from an anti-aircraft projectile. The signal for the air raid had been ordered some minutes before, and it is thought that your husband, instead of going to the ground floor of the Pier Hotel, may have gone by mistake with those detailed to use the public shelter outside.

It is terribly sad to think that his death should have been caused in this way, but I know you will realise how dangerous it is when buts of shell and shrapnel are in the air during an air raid attack.

May I before closing express my sincere sympathy in your great loss.

Yours sincerely,

H. Monroe

VICE ADMIRAL.

The reply just added to the mystery, and became yet another contradictory story . . .

Note the differences to the Chaplain's eye witness account.

1. I have seen the *report* of your husband's death.
2. He was found in a state of collapse under the fire escape *of the block of flats adjacent to* the Pier Hotel.
3. It is not certain how this came about.
4. . . . your husband, instead of going to the ground floor of the Pier Hotel *may have gone by mistake with those detailed* to use the public shelter.

The line which reads "you will realise how dangerous it is when bits of shell and shrapnel are in the air" sounds almost like a reprimand – or what do you expect, going out in the open air during an air raid?

It is perfectly clear that both accounts (the Chaplain's and the Naval Vice Admiral's) contain serious contradictions. The Chaplain claims to have been with him – "We were all making our way to the shelters". That *we* was Chick and other officers going through their routine drill, so he could never have made a mistake, nor "been found" later – and why attempt to go to a civilian shelter outside of the hotel, when the outside emergency stairs were the hotel's, and ended in a private yard belonging to the hotel. In other words, he could not vacate the hotel from the top floor, via the outside emergency stairs and end up anywhere else other than inside the hotel's yard – which is exactly what the Chaplain said. He saw him "fall unconscious" – so how could he be "found" later when the Chaplain and others picked him up and carried him into the rear of the hotel, which was only four yards from the foot of the stairs?

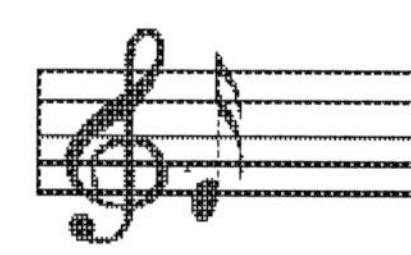

POSTSCRIPT

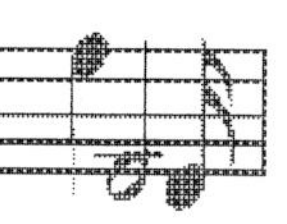

The usual speculation went on in later years about Chick. What would have happened if he had survived?

"He would have rivalled Sinatra!"

"He would have been a big Star!!"

"He would have been a great TV personality!"

. . . and so on.

They said the same about Al Bowlly – and others, but we all know what happened to our other "No. 1 Dance Band Singers" like Sam Browne, who had ended up as a counter clerk in a betting shop when I interviewed him in 1964.

In the case of Chick, it is doubtful if he would have returned to the very risky post-war entertainment scene. Dance Bands were on the way out by the end of the 1940's, but Chick had made a success of his new career in the Royal Navy. Who would want to exchange a successful career as Sub-Lieutenant (and he was studying to go further) for a 'hitty-missy' job as a Palais crooner?

His wife told me:

"I cannot speak on behalf of Chick, but looking back to those days and projecting my thoughts forward, I know that Chick would not have returned to Joe Loss and his Orchestra. He had made the break and was doing quite nicely as far as his entertainment work was going, with the occasional broadcast arranged by the Royal Navy. Indeed, the day after he was killed, this letter addressed to Chick arrived at the house."

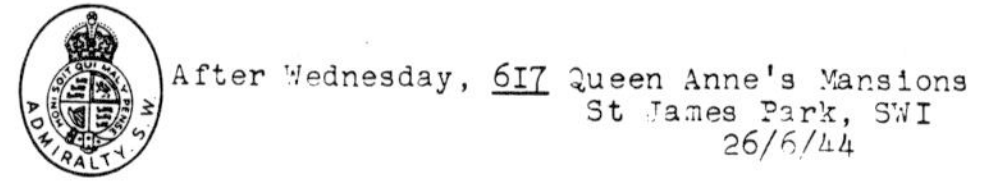

ADMIRALTY S.W.

After Wednesday, 617 Queen Anne's Mansions
St James Park, SWI
26/6/44

Dear Chick,

Many thanks for your letter of a week ago and many congratulations on getting your commission. You've done it the hard way and every credit is due to you. I hope things continue to go well for you and that we shall still be able to get you up for our programmes.

An official request went off for you to the Commodore, R.N.B. to come up for some 'Composer Cavalcade' programmes on p.m. of July IOth and all day IIth & I2th. These are lovely shows with a big orchestra, each programme being devoted to the music of one particular composer. So I hope it comes off all right.

I hope you are not being annoyed by these flying pests. We're getting a bit bored with them here.

See you on the IIth I hope as I shall try to look in,

Ever sincerely,

A.C. [signature]

Lieut-Comdr RNVR
Personal Services Dept

"From the letter, it is easy to note that Chick enjoyed appearing as a Naval Officer on Services programmes. I would go so far as to say that Chick was more interested in the Royal Navy than he was in singing with dance bands. Sometimes I have no doubt in my mind that Chick would have stayed in the Royal Navy and made a good career for himself. He was an excellent technician and was studying to become a fully fledged Lieutenant. Many of the 'high-ups' in the Royal Navy were fond of him, and saw in him a very useful person for the Service. Apart from being a very competent expert on ships' engines, he was able to communicate this knowledge to those who needed to be instructed.

There are those who would say that, because I was more proud of his war record and achievements in the Royal Navy, that this is wishful thinking on my behalf. However, I was his wife and I knew him perhaps better than his own family, for, whatever his ambitions were when he was single and singing with a peacetime 'Palais' Band, the Chick that I knew during the war was proud to be in the Royal Navy – and I could see his new future taking shape more and more each day."

Perhaps the Chick Henderson Story ended for us in 1942 when he made his last record, "What more can I say?"

The story of Sub-Lieutenant Henderson Rowntree, R.N.V.R., definitely ended on 25th June, 1944!

This scroll commemorates
Sub-Lieutenant (E) H. Rowntree
Royal Naval Volunteer Reserve
held in honour as one who
served King and Country in
the world war of 1939-1945
and gave his life to save
mankind from tyranny. May
his sacrifice help to bring
the peace and freedom for
which he died.

CHICK HENDERSON

A COMPLETE DISCOGRAPHY

MATRIX No.	RECORD MAKE & NUMBER	TITLE
Recorded in the REX STUDIOS, Broadhurst Gardens, London, with HARRY LEADER AND HIS BAND.		
25th June, 1935		
2544-1	ECLIPSE 8" 1011	Zing went the strings of my heart
2545-1	ECLIPSE 8" 1011	You filled my heart with sunshine
2546-1	ECLIPSE 8" 1010	The Little golden locket
EMI STUDIOS, St. John's Wood, London, with HARRY LEADER and his Band.		
10th September, 1935		
CA 15223-1	COLUMBIA FB 1144	You're all that I need
CA 15224-1	COLUMBIA FB 1144	Linda
EMI STUDIOS, St. John's Wood, London, with JOE LOSS and his Orchestra.		
22nd October, 1935		
OEA 1998-1	HMV BD293	Wyoming in the gloaming
OEA 2000-1	HMV BD293	The General's fast asleep
OEA 2001-1	HMV BD294	For you, madonna
EMI STUDIOS, St. John's Wood, London, with HARRY LEADER and his Band.		
6th November, 1935		
CA 15433-1	COLUMBIA FB 1218	Just as long as the world goes round
EMI STUDIOS, St. John's Wood, London, with JOE LOSS and his Orchestra.		
12th December, 1935		
OEA 2645-1	HMV BD5007	When Budapest was young
OEA 2647-1	HMV BD5008	Stardust covered bundle
OEA 2648-1	HMV BD5008	My shadow's where my sweetheart used to be.
EMI STUDIOS, St. John's Wood, London, with JOE LOSS and his Orchestra.		
13th February, 1936		
OEA 2901-1	HMV BD5036	Looking forward to looking after you
OEA 2904-1	HMV BD5036	Log cabin lullaby
21st April, 1936		
OEA 2772-1	HMV BD5064	Spread it abroad
OEA 2775-2	HMV BD5064	You started me dreaming
4th June, 1936		
OEA 3803-1	HMV BD5079	At the close of a long, long day
OEA 3804-2	HMV BD5080	Madame - ah - la Marquise - ah (with unknown female)

MATRIX No.	RECORD MAKE & NUMBER	TITLE
10th July, 1936		
OEA 3834-1	HMV BD5084	Got to dance my way to heaven
OEA 3835-1	HMV BD5084	The scene changes
OEA 3836-1	HMV BD5085	When the swallows nest again
10th September, 1936		
OEA 3853-1	HMV BD5110	Until tomorrow
OEA 3854-1	HMV BD5110	There's a new world

EMI STUDIOS, St. John's Wood, London, with HARRY LEADER and his Band.

MATRIX No.	RECORD MAKE & NUMBER	TITLE
7th October, 1936		
CA 15969-1	COLUMBIA FB1550	I'm forever blowing bubbles (part of medley)
CA 15970-1	COLUMBIA FB1532	Blaze away (part of vocal trio)

EMI STUIDOS, St. John's Wood, London, with JOE LOSS and his Orchestra.

MATRIX No.	RECORD MAKE & NUMBER	TITLE
10th October, 1936		
OEA 4072-1	HMV BD5123	I breathe on windows
OEA 4073-1	HMV BD5124	When the poppies bloom again
OEA 4074-1	HMV BD5124	Raindrops

EMI STUDIOS, St. John's Wood, London, with JOE LOSS and his Band

MATRIX No.	RECORD MAKE & NUMBER	TITLE
7th November, 1936		
CAR 4306-2	RZ MR-2263	When did you leave Heaven?
CAR 4307-1	RZ MR-2263	You've got to blow your own trumpet
CAR 4312-1	RZ MR-2274	Medley (Waltzes) It's a sin to tell a lie (vocal)
CAR 4311-1	RZ MR-2274	Medley (Foxtrots) When the poppies bloom again (vocal)
17th November, 1936		
CAR 4316-1	RZ MR-2313	Pennies from Heaven
CAR 4318-1	RZ MR-2313	So do I
CAR 4319-1	RZ MR-2283	Did you mean it?
7th January, 1937		
CAR 4376-1	RZ MR-2315	May I have the next romance with you?
CAR 4377-1	RZ MR-2314	In the Chapel in the moonlight
CAR 4379-1	RZ MR-2314	Here's love in your eye

EMI STUDIOS, St. John's Wood, London, with Wally Bishop and his Band (really Harry Leader and his Band).

MATRIX No.	RECORD MAKE & NUMBER	TITLE
14th January, 1937		
CAR 4384-1	RZ MR-2324	Another perfect night is ending
CAR 4385-1	RZ MR-2324	My heart is full of sunshine
CAR 4386-1	RZ MR-2325	The memory of a tiny shoe
CAR 4387-1	RZ MR-2325	Sentimental Fool
CAR 4388-1	RZ MR-2326	Happy dreams, Happy times, Goodnight
CAR 4389-1	RZ MR-2326	Sailor, where art thou?

MATRIX No.	RECORD MAKE & NUMBER	TITLE

EMI STUDIOS, St. John's Wood, London, with JOE LOSS and his Band.

2nd February, 1937

CAR 4425-1	RZ MR-2351	Let's dance at the make-believe ballroom (as part of trio)
CAR 4426-1	RZ MR-2351	Sweet Sue - Just You

From this point on, all recordings made at EMI STUDIOS, St. John's Wood, London (unless otherwise stated).

With WALLY BISHOP and his Band (really Harry Leader!)

6th February, 1937

CAR 4440-1	RZ MR-2357	Turning the town upside down
CAR 4441-1	RZ MR-2357	Looking around corners for you

With JOE LOSS and his Band.

27th February, 1937

CAR 4451-1	RZ MR-2390	Goodnight my love
CAR 4452-1	RZ MR-2390	The night is young, and you're so beautiful
CAR 4453-1	RZ MR-2391	A nice cup of tea

1st April, 1937

CAR 4504-1	RZ MR-2434	Let's put our heads together
CAR 4505-1	RZ MR-2434	With plenty of money and you
CAR 4506-1	RZ MR-2421	Sweet Leilani
CAR 4507-1	RZ MR-2422	Red, White and Blue
CAR 4509-1	RZ MR-2422	Across the Great Divide

5th May, 1937

CAR 4546-1	RZ MR-2450	Keep calling me sweetheart
CAR 4547-1	RZ MR-2450	With a twinkle in your eye

5th June, 1937

CAR 4578-1	RZ MR-2464/ MR-2530	September in the Rain
CAR 4579-1	RZ MR-2464	On a little dream ranch
CAR 4581-1	RZ MR-2465	They can't take that away from me

29th June, 1937

CAR 4595-1	RZ MR-2486	I saw a ship a-sailing
CAR 4596-1	RZ MR-2484	In a little French Casino
CAR 4597-1	RZ MR-2484	A Sailboat in the Moonlight

10th July, 1937

CAR 4616-1	RZ MR-2510/ MR-2530	It looks like rain in Cherry Blossom Lane

MATRIX No.	RECORD MAKE & NUMBER	TITLE
With JOE LOSS and his Band.		
13th July, 1937		
CAR 4603-1	RZ MR-2483	Shall we Dance - Selection Part 1, includes *"They can't take that away from me".*
CAR 4604-1	RZ MR-2483	Shall we Dance - Selection Part 2, includes *"Beginner's Luck".*
CAR 4623-1	RZ MR-2509	On the Avenue Selection, includes *"You're laughing at me".*
SOLO VOCALS with piano and accordeon.		
20th July, 1937		
CAR 4627-1	RZ MR-2516	Greatest mistake of my life
CAR 4628-1	RZ MR-2516	Broken hearted clown
With JOE LOSS and his Band.		
4th September, 1937		
CAR 4651-1	RZ MR-2528	Stardust on the moon
CAR 4652-1	RZ MR-2527	I know now
CAR 4653-1	RZ MR-2528	Home Town
CAR 4654-1	RZ MR-2527	So rare
8th October, 1937		
CAR 4684-1	RZ MR-2554	Mine alone
CAR 4689-1	RZ MR-2553	Whispers in the dark
28th October, 1937		
CAR 4720-1	RZ MR-2609	The moon got in my eyes
CAR 4721-1	RZ MR-2609	It's the natural thing to do
CAR 4722-1	RZ MR-2608	Little old lady
CAR 4723-1	RZ MR-2608	In the Mission by the sea
5th November, 1937		
CAR 4724-1	RZ MR-2610	That old feeling
CAR 4726-1	RZ MR-2610	You can't stop me from dreaming
20th November, 1937		
CAR 4748-1	RZ MR-2639	I still love to kiss you goodnight
CAR 4749-1	RZ MR-2639	Remember me?
Solo records accompanied by the JOE LOSS BAND.		
20th November, 1937		
CAR 4750-1	RZ MR-2617	Old pal of mine
CAR 4751-2	RZ MR-2617	After all these years

MATRIX No.	RECORD MAKE & NUMBER	TITLE
With JOE LOSS and his Band.		
2nd December, 1937		
CAR 4772-1	RZ MR-2646	Waterlilies in the moonlight
CAR 4773-1	RZ MR-2646	Roses in december
CAR 4774-1	RZ MR-2645	Sailing home
11th December, 1937		
CAR 4804-1	RZ MR-2657	Nice work if you can get it
CAR 4807-1	RZ MR-2657	A foggy day
8th January, 1938		
CAR 4823-1	RZ MR-2665	Once in a while
CAR 4824-1	RZ MR-2665	When I heard the organ play
CAR 4825-1	RZ MR-2666	Bei mir bist du schoen
With HARRY LEADER and his Band.		
11th January, 1938		
CA 16784-1	COL FB-1878	Vieni, Vieni
With JOE LOSS and his Band.		
5th February, 1938		
CAR 4843-1	RZ MR-2695	The Girl in the Alice Blue Gown
CAR 4844-1	R Z MR-2694	I double dare you
CAR 4845-1	RZ MR-2695	The pretty little patchwork quilt
CAR 4846-1	RZ MR-2694	Rosalie
10th March, 1938		
CAR 4891-1	RZ MR-2715	In my little red book
CAR 4892-1	RZ MR-2715	With you
CAR 4893-1	RZ MR-2716	Goodnight, sweet dreams, goodnight
CAR 4894-1	RZ MR-2716	Tears in my heart
With HARRY LEADER and his Band.		
15th March, 1938		
CA 16877-1	COL FB-1926	Trusting my luck
CA 16879-1	COL FB-1927	London is saying goodnight
With JOE LOSS and his Band.		
9th April, 1938		
CAR 4970-1	RZ MR-2741	"Snow White and the Seven Dwarfs" selection includes *"With a smile and a Song".*
CAR 4971-1	RZ MR-2742	By an old pagoda
CAR 4972-1	RZ MR-2742	You're an education

MATRIX No.	RECORD MAKE & NUMBER	TITLE
7th May, 1938		
CAR 5003-1	RZ MR-2762	Our old home
CAR 5004-1	RZ MR-2763	Goodnight, angel
CAR 5005-1	RZ MR-2763	You got the best of the bargain
8th June, 1938		
CAR 5018-1	RZ MR-2787	Please be kind
CAR 5019-1	RZ MR-2785	Love walked In
CAR 5020-1	RZ MR-2786	When the organ played "Oh promise me"
CAR 5021-1	RZ MR-2786	The girl in the upstairs flat
4th July, 1938		
CAR 5046-1	RZ MR-2805	Outside of paradise
CAR 5047-1	RZ MR-2806	I can dream, can't I?
CAR 5048-1	RZ MR-2823	Summer Hits Medley, includes - *"Tears in my Heart".*
16th July, 1938		
CAR 5061-1	RZ MR-2825	Throw another log on the Fire
CAR 5062-1	RZ MR-2825	Little lady make believe
CAR 5064-1	RZ MR-2826	Just let me look at you
20th August, 1938		
CAR 5089-1	RZ MR-2846	On the sentimental side
CAR 5091-1	RZ MR-2846	Music, Maestro, please
1st October, 1938		
CAR 5114-1	RZ MR-2864	Now it can be told
CAR 5116-1	RZ MR-2863	Alexander's Ragtime Band - Film Medley includes *"Easter Parade".*
CAR 5117-1	RZ MR-2863	Alexander's Ragtime Band - Film Medley includes *"Now it can be Told".*
8th October, 1938		
CAR 5124-1	RZ MR-2872	In a Little toy sailboat
CAR 5125-1	RZ MR-2872	There goes my affection
CAR 5126-1	RZ MR-2873	Never break a promise
CAR 5127-1	RZ MR-2873	Cinderella (Stay in my arms)
29th October, 1938		
CAR 5144-1	RZ MR-2920	Change partners
CAR 5147-1	RZ MR-2906	You go to my head
7th November, 1938		
CAR 5163-1	RZ MR-2920	Heart and soul
CAR 6165-1	RZ MR-2922/ MR-2939	When Mother Nature sings her lullaby

MATRIX No.	RECORD MAKE & NUMBER	TITLE
3rd December, 1938		
CAR 5196-1	RZ MR-2937	While a cigarette was burning
CAR 5197-1	RZ MR-2938	Two sleepy people
CAR 5199-1	RZ MR-2938	Honey Chile
30th December, 1938		
CAR 5225-1	RZ MR-2959	My own
CAR 5227-1	RZ MR-2958	The Umbrella man
7th January, 1939		
CAR 5228-1	RZ MR-2965	All ashore
CAR 5240-1	RZ MR-2965	Day after day
21st January, 1939		
CAR 5258-1	RZ MR-2992/ MR-2999	You must have been a beautiful baby
2nd February, 1939		
CAR 5263-1	RZ MR-2989	Tears on my pillow
CAR 5264-1	RZ MR-2989	I shall always remember you smiling
CAR 5265-1	RZ MR-2990	Grandma said
CAR 5266-1	RZ MR-2990	Romany
7th March, 1939		
CAR 5287-1-	RZ MR-2997/ HMV JH-24	The Park Parade
CAR 5288-1	RZ MR-2998	I miss you in the morning
CAR 5306-1	RZ MR-3011	The same old story
9th March, 1939		
CAR 5302-1	RZ MR-3009	Hurry home
CAR 5304-1	RZ MR-3010	Home at sundown
CAR 5305-1	RZ MR-3011	Between a kiss and a sigh
5th April, 1939		
CAR 5358-1	RZ MR-3030	Deep purple
CAR 5359-1	RZ MR-3030	Thanks for everything
CAR 5360-1	RZ MR-3031	I Promise you
CAR 5361-1	RZ MR-3031	Hold tight
6th April, 1939		
CAR 5370-1	RZ MR-3033	The Blackbird Hop
CAR 5371-1	RZ MR-3033	The Palais Stroll *(introduced by Joe Loss)*

MATRIX No.	RECORD MAKE & NUMBER	TITLE
8th May, 1939		
CAR 5396-1	RZ MR-3048	Little Sir Echo (with Monte Rey)
CAR 5398-1	RZ MR-3049	I paid for the lie that I told you
CAR 5399-1	RZ MR-3049	Poor contrary Mary
10th May, 1939		
CAR 5401-1	RZ MR-3057	This night (will be my souvenir)
9th June, 1939		
CAR 5434-1	RZ MR-3073	And the angels sing
CAR 5435-1	RZ MR-3073	Our love
CAR 5436-1	RZ MR-3073	The pretty little Quaker girl
5th July 1939		
CAR 5468-1	RZ MR-3097	That sly old gentleman
CAR 5469-1	RZ MR-3098	Begin the beguine
CAR 5470-1	RZ MR-3098	My prayer (Avant de mourir)
8th July, 1939		
CAR 5471-1	RZ MR-3097	Sing a song of sunbeams
CAR 5476-1	RZ MR-3114	There's something wrong with the weather
CAR 5477-1	RZ MR-3112	Tears from my Inkwell
CAR 5478-1	RZ MR-3114	Why begin again?
CAR 5479-1	RZ MR-3112	I never knew Heaven could speak
17th July, 1939		
CAR 5488-1	RZ MR-3113	Shabby old cabby
9th September, 1939		
CAR 5492-1	RZ MR-3135	Moon love
CAR 5493-1	RZ MR-3133	I poured my heart into a song
CAR 5494-1	RZ MR-3135	Serenade in blue
CAR 5495-1	RZ MR-3134	Drifting down the river of dreams
CAR 5496-1	RZ MR-3134	Well, all right (Tonight's the Night)
CAR 5505-1	RZ MR-3133	Run, rabbit, run!

CAR 5469/70 issued in Holland on "GLORIA" GZ 3275 deleted May 1942 also in India on "TWIN" FT 8755 in December 1939, also Australia in December 1957 on 45 EA 4320 where CAR 5470 was coupled with OEA 9426

A shellac of CAR 5470 was re-cut as 7TEA 1997 for an EP and the Master was destroyed 7th October, 1964.

MATRIX No.	RECORD MAKE & NUMBER	TITLE
6th October, 1939		
CAR 5510-1	RZ MR-3139	We're gonna hang out the washing on the Siegfried Line
CAR 5511-1	RZ MR-3139	And that started it
CAR 5514-1	RZ MR-3151	Sweet Fanny Adams' Daughter (dialogue with Joe Loss)
CAR 5515-1	RZ MR-3151	How ashamed I was!
CAR 5516-1	RZ MR-3146	Old Soldiers Never Die - Part 1 includes *"It's a Long Way to Tipperary".*
CAR 5517-1	RZ MR-3146	Old Soldiers Never Die - Part 2 includes *"If you were the only girl in the world".*
With MEL ROSE and his Orchestra (really Joe Loss)		
11th October, 1939		
CAR 5524-1	RZ MR-3153	Wish me luck (as you wave me goodbye)
CAR 5525-1	RZ MR-3153	A man and his dream
With JOE LOSS and his Band		
CAR 5528-1	RZ MR-3159	Ridin' home
CAR 5520-1	RZ MR-3159	Oh, you crazy moon
2nd November, 1939		
CAR 5557-1	RZ MR-3174	The night that you were born
CAR 5558-1	RZ MR-3174	Love never grows old
CAR 5560-1	RZ MR-3175	Blue orchids
4th November, 1939		
CAR 5559-1	RZ MR-3175/ MR-3186	Till the lights of London shine again
With MEL ROSE and his Orchestra (really Joe Loss)		
4th November, 1939		
CAR 5561-1	RZ MR-3179	Berlin or Bust
CAR 5563-1	RZ MR-3176	We must all stick together
CAR 5564-1	RZ MR-3176	Oh, ain't it grand to be in the Navy
With JOE LOSS and his Band.		
18th November, 1939		
CAR 5590-1	RZ MR-3187	The Black Out Stroll
CAR 5591-1	RZ MR-3200/ MR-3230	Somewhere in France with you
CAR 5593-1	RZ MR-3187	I'll remember
8th December, 1939		
CAR 5605-1	RZ MR-3199	Scatterbrain
CAR 5606-1	RZ MR-3199	Goodnight, children, everywhere *(with Shirley Lenner)*
CAR 5607-1	RZ MR-3200	We'll meet again
CAR 5609-1	RZ MR-3201	Day In, day out

MATRIX No.	RECORD MAKE & NUMBER	TITLE
28th December, 1939		
CAR 5631-1	RZ MR-3204	I shall be waiting
CAR 5632-1	RZ MR-3205	Are you havin' any fun? (with two others)
3rd January, 1940		
CAR 5648-1	RZ MR-3216	Good Morning (Trio includes Chick}
CAR 5649-1	RZ MR-3216	Where or when
CAR 5650-1	RZ MR-3217	Bella bambina
CAR 5651-1	RZ MR-3217	Give me my ranch
4th January, 1940		
CAR 5652-1	RZ MR-3218	Somewhere at sea
CAR 5653-1	RZ MR-3218	When Penelope Prim passes by
18th January, 1940		
CAR 5662-1	RZ MR-3244	I'm in love for the last time
CAR 5653-1	RZ MR-3232	It's a Hap-Hap-Happy Day (with two others)
19th January, 1940		
CAR 5666-1	RZ MR-3230	Rosita (Her name was Rosita)

With MEL ROSE and his Orchestra (really Joe Loss).

19th January, 1940		
CAR 5667-1	RZ MR-3231	Goodnight, my beautiful
CAR 5668-1	RZ MR-3231	Fare thee Well

With JOE LOSS and his Band.

19th January, 1940		
CAR 5669-1	RZ MR-3232	The Gaucho serenade
15th February, 1940		
CAR 5682-1	RZ MR-3248	It's a lovely day tomorrow
CAR 5683-1	RZ MR-3248	Seventeen candles
CAR 5686-1	RZ MR-3250	Let the people sing
CAR 5687-1	RZ MR-3250	Safe in my heart
29th February, 1940		
CAR 5692-1	RZ MR-3249	Who's taking you home tonight?
CAR 5693-1	RZ MR-3249	Careless
CAR 5699-1	RZ MR-3261	When you wear your sunday blue
8th March, 1940		
CAR 5690-1	RZ MR-3260	When you wish upon a star
CAR 5701-1	RZ MR-3261	Put that down in writing
CAR 5703-1	RZ MR3262	A little rain must fall
CAR 5704-1	RZ MR3262	A small cafe by Notre Dame

CAR 5699 was issued in Holland on GLORIA GZ3312 and deleted in May 1942.

MATRIX No.	RECORD MAKE & NUMBER	TITLE
With JOE LOSS and his Orchestra.		
20th March, 1940		
OEA 8392-1	HMV BD-5578	Walkin' thru' Mockin' Bird Lane
OEA 8393-1	HMV BD-5579	In an old Dutch garden
1st May, 1940		
OEA 8589-1	HMV BD-5588	Let the curtain come down
OEA 8590-1	HMV BD-5588	You made me care
OEA 8591-1	HMV BD-5589	The Woodpecker song
OEA 8592-1	HMV BD-5589	If I should fall in love again
28th May, 1940		
OEA 8674-1	HMV BD-5598	In a Little rocky valley
OEA 8675-1	HMV BD-5597	The singing hills
With the JOE LOSS Concert Orchestra.		
31st May, 1940		
OEA 8677-1	HMV BD-5599	The Navy's here
OEA 8678-1	HMV BD-5599	The Grandest song of all
With JOE LOSS and his Orchestra.		
21st June, 1940		
OEA 8811-1	HMV BD-5604	When I dream of Home
OEA 8812-1	HMV BD-5604	Moonlight and mimosa
OEA 8813-1	HMV BD-5603	Sweet little sweetheart
With HARRY ROY'S Band.		
20th August, 1940		
CAR 5851-1	RZ MR-3355	The Breeze and I
CAR 5852-1	RZ MR-3355	If you hadn't asked me to dance
CAR 5853-1	RZ MR-3354	We'll go smiling along
CAR 5854-1	RZ MR-3354	Sarah, Sarah (with Harry Roy)
With BILLY THORBURN'S - the organ, the dance band and me.		
5th September, 1940		
CE 10558-1	PAR F-1770	The Mem'ry of a rose
CE 10559-1	PAR F-1787	There'll come another day
CE 10560-1	PAR F-1787	Let the bands play
With the LONDON PIANO ACCORDEON BAND.		
18th September, 1940		
CAR 5863-1	RZ MR-3352	Turn your money in your pocket
CAR 5864-1	RZ MR-3353	When I dream of home
CAR 5865-1	RZ MR-3352	Am I for you?
CAR 5866-1	RZ MR-3353	The Memory of a Rose

CAR 5863/65 issued in India on 'TWIN' FT 8918 and in Ireland on RZ. 1Z 1088.
CAR 5864/66 issued in India on 'TWIN' FT 8914 and in Ireland on RZ. 1Z 1089.

MATRIX No.	RECORD MAKE & NUMBER	TITLE

With HARRY ROY and his Band.

20th September, 1940

CAR 5869-1	RZ MR-3373	Until you fall in love
CAR 5870-1	RZ MR-3372	All the things you are
CAR 5871-1	RZ MR-3373	I'm stepping out with a memory tonight
CAR 5872-1	RZ MR-3372	Sierra Sue

The following month, October 1940, Chick Henderson was called up for Active Service. He made the following recordings whilst on leave from the Navy.

With JOE LOSS and his Orchestra (recorded at the Kingsway Hall, London).

5th September, 1941

OEA 9508-1	HMV BD-5701	Violin
OEA 9509-1	HMV BD-5699	Dear old lady, London town
OEA 9510-1	HMV BD-5700	Pals (The Pal Song)
OEA 9512-1	HMV BD-5699	Mister Brown of London town

7th September, 1941

OEA 9511-1	HMV BD-5701	Dolores
OEA 9521-1	HMV BD-5706	Sand in my shoes

Recorded in the COLSTON HALL, BRISTOL.

21st September, 1941

OEA 9273-1-2	Rejected/Scrapped	Aurora (two takes)
OEA 9423-1	HMV BD-5707	Cornsilk
OEA 9424-1	HMV BD-5708	Marie Elena
OEA 9426-1	HMV BD-5708	Starlight serenade
OEA 9427-1	HMV BD-5706	Ridin' home on the buggy

Recorded in the EMPIRE, LEEDS.

11th December, 1941

OEA 9703-1	HMV BD-5723	Some sunny day
OEA 9705-1	HMV BD-5724	Ma-Ma-Maria
OEA 9707-1	HMV BD-5725	There's a land of begin again

12th December, 1941

OEA 9704-1	HMV BD-5724	You're in my arms
OEA 9706-1	HMV BD-5725	Rancho pillow

Recorded at GREEN'S PLAYHOUSE, GLASGOW.

9th January, 1942

OEA 9723-1	HMV BD-5734	Baby mine
OEA 9724-1	HMV BD-5734	When I see an Elephant Fly
OEA 9728-1	HMV BD-5735	Concerto for two

MATRIX No.	RECORD MAKE & NUMBER	TITLE
10th January, 1942		
OEA 9722-1	HMV BD-5729	My paradise
OEA 9727-1	HMV BD-5729	That lovely weekend
OEA 9729-1	HMV BD-5735	What more can I say?

Chick Henderson
was accidentally killed
by a piece of shrapnel
from a
British Ack-Ack gun,
which was firing at
German V2 pilotless bombers
over Southsea
on 25th June, 1944.

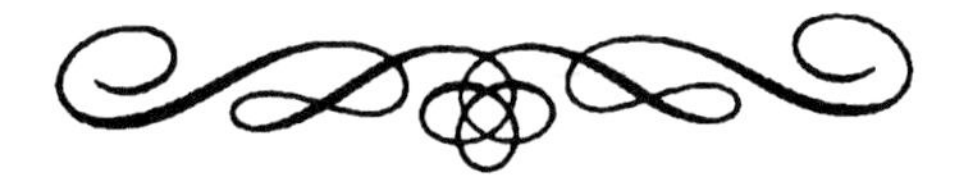

At the time of going to press, there have been three L.P.'s of Chick Henderson issued in Australia, and a fourth, including a compact disc, is in the pipeline.

None have been issued in the U.K. at the time of publication.

The nearest the U.K. got was an E.P. in 1964, and an L.P. giving first credit (again) to Joe Loss.

The Chick Henderson Appreciation Society plans to have its own re-issues to make up for the deficiency and to have, also, a quarterly magazine.

For further details, please write to:

Chick Henderson Appreciation Society,
c/o Frank Wappat,
Church House,
Drummond Terrace,
NORTH SHIELDS,
NE30 2DL.